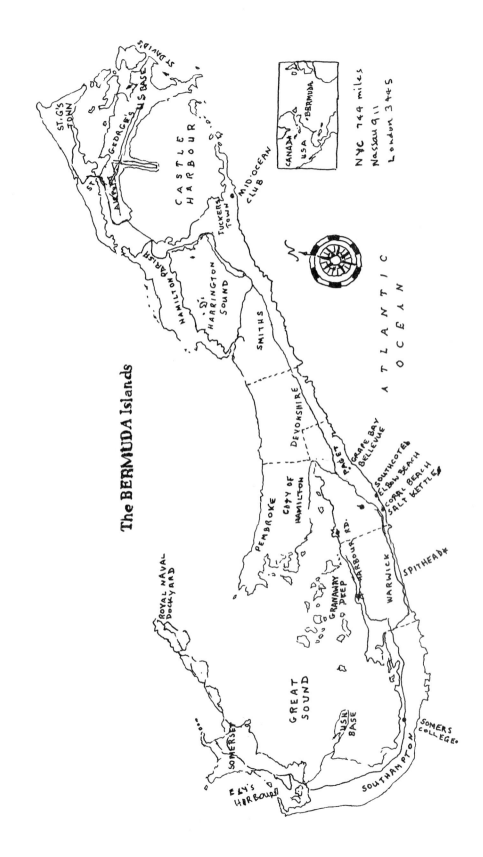

The BERMUDA Islands

NYC 744 miles
Nassau 911
London 3 + 5

ST. G'S JOHN

ST. DAVIDS

ST. GEORGE'S US BASE

AIRPORT

CASTLE HARBOUR

MID OCEAN CLUB

TUCKERS TOWN

HAMILTON PARISH

HARRINGTON SOUND

SMITHS

DEVONSHIRE

ATLANTIC OCEAN

GRAPE BAY
BELLEVUE

SOUTHCOTE
ELBOW BEACH
CORAL BEACH
SALT KETTLE

PAGET

HARBOUR RD.

WARWICK

SPITHEAD

CITY OF HAMILTON

PEMBROKE

ROYAL NAVAL DOCKYARD

GRANAWAY DEEP

USN BASE

GREAT SOUND

SOMERSET

ELY'S HARBOUR

SOUTHAMPTON

SOMERS COLLEGE

CANADA
USA
BERMUDA

WITH the dwelling-house erected on the parcel of land marked "A"
on the said plan known as "Spithead" and all other buildings
fixtures ways rights-of-way liberties privileges easements
advantages and appurtenances whatsoever to the said parcels of
land or any of them belonging or in anywise appertaining or
usually held or occupied therewith or reputed to belong or
be appurtenant thereto.

Signed Sealed and Delivered)
by the above named Eugene
Gladstone O'Neill in the
presence of:

Signed Sealed and Delivered)
by the above named Agnes
Boulton Kaufman in the
presence of:

Signed Sealed and Delivered)
by the above named Oona
O'Neill Chaplin in the
presence of:

Signed Sealed and Delivered)
by the above named Shane
O'Neill in the presence of:)

Signed Sealed and Delivered)
by the above named Charles
Spencer Chaplin in the
presence of:

$25,000.00
Received on the day of the date of the above written Indenture
from the within named Joel Cook Huber and Mary Hays Huber the
sum of Twenty-five thousand dollars within mentioned to be
paid to me the sum of Eight pounds nineteen shillings in postage and
revenue stamps having been previously hereto affixed for stamp
duty.

Witnesses to the signature
of Agnes Boulton Kaufman

A page from the Spithead deeds has the signatures of Eugene O'Neill,
Agnes, Oona, Shane and Charlie Chaplin. The Bermuda stamps show the
duty payable on the sale of the property in 1952.

Eugene O'Neill and Family

❦

The Bermuda Interlude

Joy Bluck Waters

Joy Bluck Waters

To Susie and Richard

Printed in Canada by
University of Toronto Press Incorporated
Toronto

ISBN 0-9696373-06

Contents

The line drawings at the beginning of each chapter and that of Campsea on page 14 are by the author.

Deeds page shown in the Frontispiece is signed by O'Neill family and Charlie Chaplin.

Preface

When I bought the eighteenth century house, Spithead, I knew that Eugene O'Neill had owned it. I also knew he was an American playwright and remembered seeing, years earlier, his waterfront play *Anna Christie*, as a movie, starring Greta Garbo. My knowledge of O'Neill was limited to say the least! The family owned the house for some twenty-six years and some of the land until recent times, so many Bermudians knew them and would tell me extraordinary tales.

I embarked on the awesome adventure of reading O'Neill's plays. *Long Day's Journey Into Night* was the only one I had at the time, so into that gloomy tale of his family's unrelenting misfortunes, I plunged. I went on and liked his early seafaring plays and then was ready to read, with particular interest, the dramas he worked on in Bermuda. As his own life became known to me I could see the price a genius pays to leave a great legacy for people everywhere and for his country. O'Neill's dedication to work was unbelievable and inevitably his wives and children suffered. In his writings he protested that the very idea of causing anyone to suffer was repugnant to him but somehow they all seemed caught up in a huge web. He half believed in cursed families. Melancholia, alcohol, illness and drugs played their part.

On the trail of O'Neill I was fortunate when my friends in New Haven, Connecticut, asked me to stay. Yale University houses most of O'Neill writings in the Beinecke Library of Rare Books and Manuscripts and is the executor of his literary estate. After lunching at Mory's, I was taken to the Beinecke where the then-curator, Dr. David Schoonover, took me under his wing. I was given letters, diaries and poems to read and told about books and biographies that were written about the dramatist and his family. I received much kindness at the Houghton Theatre Collection at Harvard where I read Agnes' loving letters to her husband during their nine years of marriage. The Berg Collection at New York Library allowed me to see their O'Neill material.

The Bermuda stories, I was told, were important because they were previously unknown. I returned from august places where I had received help from many knowledgeable people, to set the tales in the context of the period the family lived in on the Island. I am most grateful to my fellow Bermudians who shared their memories with me. They are from all walks of life and told me about their association with the O'Neills and the amazing events that occurred. I was not acquainted with all of them at first and it was a rich experience getting to know them. Many of them are very old now but they have remarkably clear memories of what happened more than half a century ago. During the twelve years it took to accumulate the stories I have to regretfully report that some have died. I am so glad their memories live on. Without everybody who helped, this book would not have been possible and whatever interest it has or pleasure it gives is largely due to them.

This is not an academic work but rather a glimpse of the lives of the great dramatist and his family, in a time of accomplishments and sorrows set against the tranquil beauty of the island. One young person who read the manuscript said it made her want to know more about O'Neill. I would be so glad if other young people, and indeed some older ones too, feel the same.

It has been believed for two hundred years that gold is buried somewhere at Spithead. Before the days of safety deposit boxes gold was often buried and sometimes the owner would die taking the secret of the whereabouts of his valuables with him. It might lie hidden for a very long time. An old man told me his father said he had seen gold taken out from the bottom of the huge water tank. O'Neill never found any that gleamed. However health is more important than gold and O'Neill who suffered from devastating alcoholism made the first serious attempts to overcome it in Bermuda. Improved health gave him the golden opportunity to do the great writing he produced here.

When the Schoonovers came to stay at Spithead we had a tea-party for some of the people who had worked on the renovations and at other jobs on the place during the O'Neills time.

Patricia Willis is now the Curator of the Beinecke and I am grateful to her for her encouragement and help with the permissions from the university for this book. Professor Jackson Bryer, one of the greatest living authorities on O'Neill, took time to encourage me and with great kindness wrote the introduction and kept me straight on facts. I am most grateful to him. They all made me feel it was worthwhile to preserve the memories of the O'Neills' Bermuda Interlude.

Joy Bluck Waters
Bermuda
August 1992

Introduction

> It was a great mistake, my being born a man, I would have been much more successful as a sea gull or a fish. As it is, I will always be a stranger who never feels at home, who does not really want and is not really wanted, who can never belong, who must always be a little in love with death!

These familiar and often-quoted lines from Eugene O'Neill's best and autobiographical play, *Long Day's Journey Into Night* not only express the ambivalences and longings of many O'Neill's protagonists, they also reflect the playwright's own deepest feelings and preoccupations. Spoken by Edmund, his alter ego in the play, they eloquently represent O'Neill's lifelong search for a literal and figurative home—a place where he can "belong"—as well as his love of the sea.

O'Neill was born on October 16, 1888, in the Barrett House, a hotel on the corner of Broadway and 43rd Street in New York City. His father, the noted actor James O'Neill, was able to spend only one night with his wife and new-born son before rushing back to New England, where he was starring as Edmond Dantes in the dramatic version of *The Count of Monte Cristo* with which he was touring the country in a series of one-night stands for the sixth consecutive year (he was to do so for twelve more years). During the first six years of his life, Eugene spent eight or nine months annually "on the road" following his father's acting troupe and his summers in New London, Connecticut, at his parents' only permanent residence, where he was frequently in the care of a nurse-maid.

When he was barely seven, he was sent to boarding school at the Academy of Mount St. Vincent in Riverdale, New York. He remained there for the next five years before transferring first, in 1900, to De La Salle Institute, a Catholic boarding school in New York City run by the Christian Brothers, and then, in 1902, to Betts Academy, a non-sectarian private boarding school in Stamford, Connecticut. After a year at Princeton University, from which he was dismissed for "poor scholastic standing," he spent the next five years "at sea"—both literally and figuratively—drifting about the globe in a variety of jobs, many of them nautical: on a gold prospecting trip to Spanish Honduras, on tramp steamers, and as an ordinary seaman on transatlantic luxury liners.

During this time, he also married, had a child by, and divorced Kathleen Jenkins. Upon his return to the United States in 1912, he briefly toured with his father's company of *Monte Cristo* before obtaining work as a reporter on the *New London Telegraph*, a job which ended abruptly when he contracted tuberculosis and was sent to a sanitarium for a year.

It was during that year that O'Neill began to read plays extensively and decided upon a career as a playwright. Subsequently, he wrote a number of one-act plays and studied playwriting with George Pierce Baker at Harvard in 1914-15. His earliest dramas were produced by the Provincetown Players, first at their Wharf Theatre in Provincetown, Massachusetts, and then at the Playwright's Theatre in New York's Greenwich Village. The success of these early ventures led eventually to his initial Broadway production, *Beyond the Horizon*, in 1920, a full-length play which won O'Neill the first of his four Pulitzer Prizes and brought him recognition as a major American dramatist and international celebrity. In 1918, he had married Agnes Boulton, herself a writer of short stories, and their son Shane was born in 1919.

Despite his success as a writer (he produced a remarkable stream of plays in the years following *Beyond the Horizon*—including *The Emperor Jones* [1920], *Diff'rent* [1920], *Gold* [1921], *Anna Christie* [1921], *The Straw* [1921], *The Hairy Ape* [1922], *All God's Chillun Got Wings* [1924], *Welded* [1924], and *Desire Under the Elms* [1924]), O'Neill remained throughout this period—and in many ways for the rest of his life— that dislocated stranger looking for a home.

Always drawn to the sea, he first settled in Provincetown, on Cape Cod, where he lived with Agnes and Shane for several years in an abandoned Coast Guard station at Peaked Hill Bar, only a few feet from the ocean. When winters there proved too severe for his family, he purchased Brook Farm in Ridgefield, Connecticut, in 1922. But he began to feel that the quality of his work declined when the weather became cooler; he regarded as his weakest the plays he had written during the winter months, while he felt he'd done his best work in warmer weather. He undoubtedly also missed being near the ocean and swimming, one of his greatest passions.

So it was that, sometime during the summer of 1924, O'Neill decided not to spend the following winter in Connecticut but, instead, to go to Bermuda. One of his biographers, Louis Shaeffer, claims that he got the idea of going to Bermuda from writer Wilbur Daniel Steele and his wife, with whom the O'Neills spent a week on Nantucket in late August. Arthur and Barbara Gelb, authors of an earlier O'Neill biography, credit Dr. Alexander Miller, a tuberculosis specialist to whom the playwright still occasionally went for check-ups, with recommending Bermuda to him.

Regardless of where the idea came from, as Joy Waters recounts, the O'Neills arrived in Bermuda on December 1, 1924. Almost exactly three years later, on November 15, 1927, Eugene O'Neill left the island for the last time. Although his stay there was frequently interrupted by trips back to the mainland, either briefly for matters relating to productions of his plays or for summers spent on Cape Cod or in Maine, he did spend approximately twenty months in the warmer climate he had sought, including three extended periods of close to six months each. And he did find the environment congenial to his creativity: while in Bermuda he did most of the work on three of his major plays—*The Great God Brown*, *Lazarus Laughed*, and *Strange Interlude*.

In Bermuda he also made the first of several attempts to establish a permanent residence; to O'Neill this meant not only a physical all-year-round house but also a place where he could find the stable—and stationary—family existence he had not had in his own early life. When, in the spring of 1926 after living in a series of rented homes, he purchased and planned extensively to renovate Spithead, he did so with the intention of creating an environment—at the water's edge and in an ever-temperate climate—which would be both creatively productive and domestically tranquil. In April 1927, shortly after finally moving in, he exulted, in a letter to Agnes, about "this haven, this ultimate island where we may rest and live toward our dreams with a sense of permanence and security that here we do belong."

But it was not to be; O'Neill's search for a place where he could "belong" was not to end in Bermuda. It was, in fact, going to continue through subsequent attempts to establish homes—in France, in Sea Island, Georgia, in California (where he and his third wife built yet another "dream house"), in Marblehead, Massachusetts—and it was to end, most ironically of all, where he had begun, on his deathbed in yet another hotel—in Boston. How and why his Bermuda idyll ended so suddenly and unexpectedly is a story worthy of one of O'Neill's own dramas, and it is part of the story Joy Waters tells here. But what she also does—and in this respect she goes well beyond all previous accounts—

is give a very precise and detailed account of what life in Bermuda was like while O'Neill lived there. Drawing from her own experience as a life-long resident of the island who now owns and lives at Spithead, as well as from interviews with persons who knew the O'Neill family in Bermuda, she recreates the atmosphere of a place which fascinated the famous playwright just as much as it does those who visit it today. Her narrative is considerably enhanced by photographs (many never before published) and her own line drawings.

Beyond giving us this informed sense of Bermuda in the 1920s, Joy Waters has also added important information to the O'Neill story. Her account of the tragic fate of O'Neill's beloved Irish wolfhound Finn McCool has never been previously reported; and because O'Neill's biographers are not concerned with what became of his wife and children after he left them, she adds valuable and fascinating material on Agnes, Shane and Oona's time in Bermuda after November 1927. Her description of Christmas 1927 is especially poignant, and her tracing of Shane's disastrous odyssey as an adult back to his boyhood home is a heretofore untold chapter in his sad life.

O'Neill's letters from Bermuda back to friends in the States are filled with his feelings of pleasure and contentment with the place and with his life there. Joy Waters's book shows us the reasons this was so. Although Bermuda ultimately was to be only a temporary resting place in O'Neill's long and tragic search for a home—for a place by the sea where he could "belong" and could achieve a peaceful and stable domestic life—it was a significant interlude. One of his Bermuda acquaintances, Montiville M. Hansford, is quoted by Shaeffer as observing about the playwright: "I believe that this man never feels quite at home with anybody...the one outstanding impression is that he does not belong anywhere." For the greater part of three years, he did feel as if he had found, in Bermuda, that home for which he had been searching all his life. Joy Waters helps us understand how and why this was so; in doing that, she fills out an important segment in the life and career of America's most important playwright.

Jackson R. Bryer
University of Maryland

Acknowledgements

To the distinguished members of some of the great institutions of the United States, who helped me and gave me access to materials, I would like to say a heartfelt thank you.

Travis Bogard, Professor Emeritus, University of California;
Jackson Bryer, Professor of American Literature, University of Maryland;
Jeanne T. Newlin, Curator of Harvard Theater Collections;
David E. Schoonover, Curator of American Literature, University of Iowa;
Lola Sladits, Curator, Berg Collection, New York, Library;
Patricia Willis, Curator, American Literature, Yale University; and
Charles T. Wood, Daniel Webster Professor of History, Dartmouth College.

Equally, I must thank my fellow Bermudians and many others who shared their memories of the O'Neill family, encouraged and helped me.

Belle Ashdown, David Ashdown, Sydney Bean, Josephine Darrell Buck, Celia Palmer Curtis, John Cox, Hilda Davis, William Davis, Timoney Foster, Donald French, Bronson Hartley, Polly Trott Hornburg, Wendy MacLeod, Peggy Anne Miller, Antoinette Frith Morris, Jack Pitt, George Powell, Eugene & Eugenia Robinson, sisters Mary Ridgway Smyth & June Ridgway Stanton, Kyril Sherbatow, Miss Simons, Edith Smith, Margaret Trott Staskow, Millicent Trott, Hereward Watlington, Charles Zuill and William Zuill.

I would like to thank Jack Arnell, for the page layouts and preparation of camera-ready copy.

Bibliography

Louis Shaeffer, *O'Neill, Playwright and Artist* (1973).

Travis Bogard & Jackson Bryer, *Selected Letters of Eugene O'Neill* (1988).

Croswell Bowen, *The Curse of the Misbegotten* (1959).

Donald Gallup, *Eugene O'Neill Work Diary* (1981).

Arthur & Barbara Gelb, *O'Neill* (1962).

Barbara Gelb, *Dictionary of American Biography*.

Sister Jean de Chantal Kennedy, *Frith of Bermuda: Gentleman Privateer* (1964).

Bruce J. Mann, *An FBI Memorandum on O'Neill E.O'N Review*.

William Zuill, *The Story of Bermuda and Her People* (1973).

Oh Wonder!
How many goodly creatures are there here!
How Beauteous mankind is! Oh brave new
world
That has such people in't!

The Tempest

Chapter 1

The O'Neills arrive by steamer at Hamilton, the capital of Bermuda.
The playwright is seeking the tranquility his genius requires.

On the first of December 1924 the S.S. *Fort St. George* sailed into Hamilton Harbour with the noted dramatist Eugene O'Neill and his family on board - not to mention his dogs. Upon landing there was immigration to clear and then their luggage had to be inspected by His Majesty's Customs, whereupon, the porters could load their bags and trunks onto a horse drawn trolley cart which would follow them to their hotel. All motor vehicles were forbidden on the Island.

O'Neill was accompanied by his beautiful wife Agnes, their five year old son Shane, Agnes' daughter Barbara by a previous marriage, Mrs. Fifine Clark the French nurse, the huge Irish wolfhound Finn Mac Cool and Bowser the bull terrier. Porters shepherded them into carriages to take them to the New Windsor Hotel on Queen Street. The trolley cart followed. Driving along through the colonial capital the scene would be a novelty for them with Victorias, Surreys with fringes on top, traps,

Two round trips a week from New York to Bermuda taking two days were
provided by the Furness steamers *Fort St. George* and *Fort Victoria*.
(*Bermuda Archives*)

wagons and bicycles thronging the thoroughfares. The roads were kept
clean by the constant efforts of the street sweepers who swept up any
horse manure, causing the sparrows feeding on the droppings to flutter
away.

Agnes O'Neill, aged thirty-one, passing along in the carriage, epito-
mized the *avant garde* of the 1920s. Photographs of the time show her
dark hair, bobbed short, and a cloche hat pulled down over her brow.
Her clothes were fashionable, her skirts shortened to above her neat
ankles. Her dresses were somewhat loose just then as she was expecting
her second O'Neill child.

O'Neill, whose reputation was ever rising, was thirty-six years old.
His thick, dark hair showed some distinguished gray and his eyes,
luminous and darkly shining, compelled attention - unforgettably -
even in the very young. (A Bermudian lady remembers them from her
childhood acquaintance with the writer.) His spare figure was strong
and he would have been in the peak of health had he not been in the
habit, as the Irish say, of "having drink taken".

The nurse, Mrs Clark, called Gaga by Shane in his infancy, affectionately retained that nickname in the O'Neill family. She was French, the
widow of an American serviceman met in France during the Great War.
A comfortable woman, she mildly shared her countrymen's traditional
dislike of the English.

The tiny city to which they had come exuded a strong English
influence, a feeling that the way of life was secure, unchangeable, there

O'Neill, Agnes and Shane in Bermuda. (*Bettmann Archives*)

"would always be an England". Every school child knew who sat on the throne in London, for he or she had to recite "I pledge allegiance to George the Fifth, Defender of the Faith, King, Emperor of India and Ruler of the British Dominions beyond the seas". The much loved Royal Family was the epitome of stability. The pound sterling which set values around the world seemed as sound as the Rock of Gibraltar.

The O'Neills had just come from their home, Brook Farm, in Ridgefield, Connecticut, to stay in Bermuda until the following summer. The young playwright was surging on a wave of success, honoured twice by winning the Pulitzer Prize. However, he was having trouble writing at Brook Farm. O'Neill liked to write day after day shut away by himself, the dog Finn on the mat and a bottle nearby in the cupboard. Agnes turned away callers seeking interviews and protected him from domestic worries. She could not protect him from himself. Temperamental and moody, anger often flaring, tension mounted when there was not the peace and continuity he needed. He fell from his Olympian heights and descended even to D.T.s. From his youth he had had tremendous bouts of drunkenness that left him depressed and debilitated. He was going down the tragic path his parents and brother knew.

O'Neill had to reconcile the two sides of his work. While he was writing a play, solitude and a place inaccessible to friends and visitors were essential but when a play went into rehearsal he had to hasten to New York and throw himself into the magical world of the theatre he loved. He had been brought up in the theatre, his father James having been a well known actor, so he was well grounded in his craft. He paid careful attention to the casting of actors for his characters, attended rehearsals and supervised scenery occasionally designing it himself.

At home, in Ridgefield, his writing days were often interrupted by friends who came out from New York and stayed. The drinks flowed and days were wasted recovering from hangovers. In spite of his hopes, Brook Farm did not provide the ideal atmosphere for his work. It was a great disappointment, especially as the place had been bought with the money from his first plays. (O'Neill and Agnes, with Shane and Gaga, had moved to Ridgefield from Provincetown. In the early days of their marriage the Provincetown Players had been the first to produce O'Neill's works. The young people there acted in American plays written by American authors and a new theatre had been born in America away from European influence.)

Struggling to overcome the frustrations he felt about his lack of seclusion at the farm, he wrote to his friend, producer and mentor, Kenneth Macgowan, "I'd like two walled acres of Siberia with a flock of Siberian wolfhounds to guard them and layers of broken glass on the walls". However, Siberia being too far away and cold besides, they decided to try the sunny shores of Bermuda, far out to sea, perfumed with flowers, a fertile rock in the Atlantic. O'Neill was in tune with the seventeenth-century poet Andrew Marvell's description of the islands:

Where the remote Bermudas ride
In the ocean's bosom unespied...

Bermuda, with its mild climate, seven hundred miles out to sea, yet only two days voyage from New York, seemed to O'Neill the ideal place at last. For Agnes, three months pregnant, it was something for her to consider: to leave her home and move to a small outpost of the British Empire. They would be there when the baby was due the following May. She adored O'Neill, though, and ever mindful of his needs, she concealed any misgivings of her own.

Before O'Neill could espy the "remote Bermudas" he wanted to finish the two-story farmhouse he was designing for the scenery of *Desire Under the Elms*. The play would become a Broadway sensation when the four rooms of the house opened to reveal to the audience how the desires of the Cabots led them to fratricide, infanticide and incest. Also to delay the O'Neills' departure was another production in rehearsal of the S.S. *Glencairn*, a popular collection of one-act plays drawn from the experiences of his youth when he shipped out on tramp steamers and windjammers. The scenes were old coalburners or waterfront taverns and the characters sailors and whores.

To add to it all a book of his plays, *Collected Works*, was to be published and he found himself involved in proof-reading. He could not wait to get away; he had been trying to find a producer for a long play, *Marco Millions*, based on the adventures of Marco Polo.

The house in Ridgefield had to be shut up and Agnes, never the organiser, got Gaga to help with what to take and what not to take, uncertain what would be needed for them abroad. The eight-year-old Barbara, who sometimes lived with Agnes' parents, would be going with them. O'Neill managed to pack his manuscripts and books, but he was away most of the time finishing up in New York. He stayed at the Lafayette Hotel, so the family moved there a few days before sailing. Heavy luggage went to the ship early with big labels saying "HOLD" and "Not wanted on the Voyage". The dogs, Finn Mac Cool and Bowser, were brought into the city and sent over to the East Side pier to be placed in the ship's kennel. Cabin trunks went over for stewards to place in readiness in the staterooms, along with any gifts and flowers, before the passengers boarded.

Leaving the hotel, there was a frantic search for mislaid tickets, the children cried but at last the playwright's caravan was off to the ship.

The boat swarmed with crowds of visitors come to see the passengers off. Drinks flowed in the cabins. Finally the stewards hurried non-travellers ashore as sailing time drew near. They called in their British voices "All ashore oo're going ashore". Bugles blew. The last tipsy visitors dashed down the gangplank as it was about to be lowered from the ship's side. The engines vibrated. The tugs pulled the ship out into the Hudson River. O'Neill could remember very different sailings from the days when he was a seaman on the old freighters.

Passengers usually stayed on deck after sailing to get a good view of the Statue of Liberty which stands on an island in New York Harbor. Mothers were advised to go down to the dining saloon to arrange their seating and the childrens' meals which were taken separately, supervised by their nurse or a patient parent. The Chief Stewart resplendent in white jacket, probably decorated with Great War medal ribbons shining on his breast, ruled over this scene of spotless napery and shining silver, the chairs chained to the deck to prevent sliding in dusty weather. No stabilisers then.

The O'Neills had hoped their arrival in Bermuda would go unnoted. Indeed, they had taken the precaution of writing ahead of time to the local paper, *The Royal Gazette and Colonist Daily*. It reported O'Neill was coming to do "much work whilst here and is therefore looking forward to peace and quiet rather than the gaieties of our season." Notoriety came however from an unexpected source. Finn Mac Cool, the Irish wolfhound, had found the small kennel on the top deck very confining and was wildly excited to be out. His dash ashore was a pearl for reporters and the *Gazette* records:

> Hamilton's business section has spent a hectic week trying to live up to Eugene O'Neill's dog, now domiciled in the New Windsor Gardens. It was observed when O'Neill's boat docked that this dog brought a steward ashore at a speed never before attained on Front Street. The Captain of the *Fort St. George* had serious intentions of manning the forward tackle and running the dog ashore in a breeches buoy, but a reckless steward volunteered to risk his life, and a rapid landing was accomplished to the great admiration of the crowd.
>
> Bermuda opinion as to his breed has run riot. The oldest inhabitant does not remember the island ever being invaded by anything like it; and the younger generation looks on in wonder. Musical persons have noticed that he bays the moon in E-flat.

When the O'Neills arrived at the New Windsor they found an inner garden courtyard where, on that December day, *bougainvillea* bloomed, palms grew, canaries sang, and the famous or infamous old parrot perched swearing in his cage. A faint aroma of rum always tickled the nose, enhancing the feeling of a colonial seaport. A wide staircase led to the verandahs above where the bedrooms lay. The O'Neills stayed there while they looked for a house to rent. They needed two, in fact, one for the family and a separate place where O'Neill could work undisturbed.

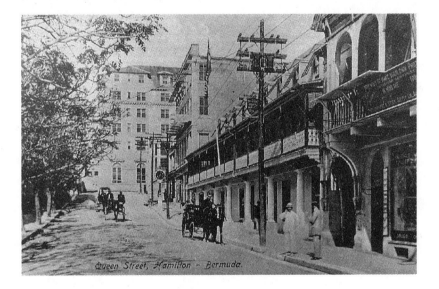

Queen Street showing the New Windsor Hotel and Gardens on the right, where the O'Neills spent their first days in Bermuda.
(*Bermuda Archives*)

It was pleasant to stay in the quiet residential town of Hamilton. Along the streets grew flowering trees and over the walls trailed vines bright with blossoms. Through the gates along the pavements could be glimpsed verandahed houses, perhaps a tennis court and a driveway leading away to stables in the rear. There was little noise in the town, so when the noonday whistle blew it could be heard everywhere, as could the town clock striking in the tower of the House of Assembly. The sounds of rumbling wheels and horses' hooves clopping came and went as did the whacking of tennis balls, voices calling the score, or the soporific clatter of a push-mower cutting the lawn.

British army officers drove through the streets in carriages, their soldier servants at the reins of their horses which sported glossy coats and polished hooves. Sailors in bellbottoms in port from Britannia's seas, tacked through Hamilton. Girls' hearts throbbed to see a handsome young naval officer, in white uniform, pass along on Admiralty business, sparing them an appreciative glance from his blue eyes, shaded by the dark peak of his white-topped cap. Most important, the Governor, the King's representative appointed from England, clattered through the capital in his landau, his feathered helmet on his head. His groom on the box drove his spirited pair through the maze of horsedrawn traffic. When the British Admiral visited the city he arrived in his navy blue barge, the yellow brass shining, the flag Officer's ensign showing the red-on-white cross of St.George.

At Government House society decreed that young ladies must wear elbow-length gloves to dinners and balls. For dinner the small pearl buttons were undone at the wrist, the hand slipped out and the empty part of the gloves neatly tucked under at the wrist out of sight. The hands of the gloves were put on again after dinner for dancing. Most children of the well-to-do were sent to England to boarding school, the boys to grow up learning to keep a stiff upper lip and to develop a good swing with a cricket bat and the girls to marry well. The interests of most Bermudians were business and sports with little time spared for the arts. There was no such thing as social integration between the white and coloured inhabitants, who later would be known as blacks.

Britain had claimed the then uninhabited coral limestone islands of Bermuda early in the seventeenth century. They lie on top of an isolated, extinct, volcanic cone, rising 18,000 feet from the ocean floor. There is a main island and about a hundred others, some islets little more than rocks. They amount to twenty square miles and are surrounded by hundreds of miles of coral reefs covering the top of the volcano. Tropical fish and plants live in the paradise among the coral heads. Many a mariner found paradise or a hotter clime, perishing in the "thousand wrecks" lying amid the reefs.

All visitors soon heard how Admiral Sir George Somers discovered the islands in 1609 when his flagship, the *Sea Venture*, was wrecked on the reefs and his fleet scattered by a great storm. He was on his way to the relief of the beleaguered colony at Jamestown, Virginia, which was stricken by illness and starvation and surrounded by hostile Indians.

The Admiral, whose ship stuck between two reefs, managed to get ashore with all his crew and tackle, and after claiming the islands for England, he set about building two ships and was able, a year later, to continue to Jamestown with produce from Bermuda. When this remarkable adventure was known in London, an account was published entitled "A discovery of the Bermudas, otherwise called the Ile of Divils". The mariners had told of haunting spirits and supernatural happenings. Archives in Cadiz show the Spaniards knew of the islands and also described them as inhabited by devils. They had not thought them worth claiming for Spain because there were no pearls or gold to be found. The islands are called after Juan Bermudez, whose name the English found carved into a rock.

In 1924 the O'Neills had found an island whose people, 24,000 in all, had the reputation of being polite and delightful. About half the population was white descended from English settlers and more recent Portuguese immigrants and the other half known as coloured were mostly descended from slaves who were freed in 1834 some ninety years before. In former times Bermudians had been boat builders and seafaring people sailing their small sloops seeking trade along the eastern seaboard of the United States, Canada and the West Indies almost a thousand miles to the south. In the mid Twenties, the tourist trade and the export of vegetables and flowers provided a living. The island's revenue was augmented by the expenditures made by the Royal Naval Dockyard and the regiment stationed in the islands from England. The colony was self-governing with an elected House of Assembly and paid no tribute to England. The island was divided into nine parishes and males, regardless of colour, were entitled to vote in any parish in which they owned property. Thus a well-to-do man could vote nine times.

By the time the O'Neills arrived, the tourist industry was burgeoning rapidly. The Furness Withy Steamship Company had just built the Bermudiana Hotel in Hamilton and two new passenger liners were on the slips in England. The exclusive Mid Ocean Club was formed and the golf course laid out by Charlie MacDonald, the "father of American golf". O'Neill called the island "tourist infested" although for a whole year tourists would only number twenty thousand then. In later years the number would reach six hundred thousand. In O'Neill's day no cars sullied the shady roads, where bicycle bells tinkled and the clopping of horses' hooves complemented the singing of cicadas in the cedar trees.

Crow's Nest

Chapter 2

The family rents cottages on a cliff by the beach.
The playwright, being very productive, writes the play
The Great God Brown.

The O'Neills started to look for a house by the sea. They wanted two, one for the family and one close by where O'Neill could work. A house agent called for them at the New Windsor in a carriage.

They drove to the south shore in the parish of Paget and there on a wild cliff with a pink-white beach far below, where the surf rolled in, stood two bungalows, "Campsea" and "Crow's Nest." Oleanders were in bloom in various shades of pink and the hibiscus opened their scarlet bells. The cliff top was wooded with shady aromatic cedars. Out to sea the great Atlantic rolled in breaking over the reef, surging on to spread a lacy edge on the sand. To the west a holiday cottage belonging to the Trott family sat sheltered in the trees. To the east at some distance stood the Elbow Beach Hotel, which could be reached by walking along the shore. The property was just what the O'Neills wanted.

The dogs were in heaven and scrambled down the cliff ahead of the family for their first swim. Bermudians respected O'Neill's desire for privacy, expressed in the *Royal Gazette*, and did not go to leave calling cards, which was their custom towards new arrivals. The land crabs who lived in burrows on top of the cliff were not so backward and came

The playwright with Bowser in Bermuda. (*Bettmann Archives*)

up to the verandah in the evening, their pincers held high in welcome. Dogs that put their noses down the crab holes got thoroughly nipped.

Safely secluded on his cliff top, O'Neill started on his first task, signing autograph sheets for the forthcoming publication of his *Collected Works*. The first edition was to be bound in white leather. The volume would contain his two Pulitzer Prize-winning plays, *Beyond the Horizon* and *Anna Christie,* both drawn from the seafaring adventures of his early life. Later on when the book was published, he gave a copy to the exiled Russian Prince Kyril and his wife Adelaide Scherbatow, new friends who lived nearby at "High Time". (Their marriage was delayed for some years waiting for the Pope to annul Adelaide's marriage, hence the name of the house.) O'Neill signed the book for them. One afternoon when the Scherbatow's guests were having drinks under the cedars by the water, Kyril brought the book out proudly to show them. Somehow it was forgotten and left out there. Tropical rain fell for several days. By the time the collector's item was discovered it was completely ruined.

O'Neill resumed work on *Marco Millions*, two plays in one with music, crowds and many scenes. It is a sumptuous account of the travels of a modern day Marco Polo, who sets out from the Palace of the Doges of Venice. He returns with fabulous treasure from the Far Eastern court of the Kublai Khan, where Princess Kukachin has fallen in love with him. The playwright records that he spent 19 days in January of '25 reducing the play to one long evening performance length.

In a notebook called *Charles Lett's Popular Scribbling Diary for 1925*, O'Neill kept a daily record of happenings. The revelations bring to light the youthful, vibrant O'Neill of the 1920s as a complement to the frequently drawn picture of the brooding literary giant, heaped with honours, associated in writing and life with tragedy. He writes about his drinking, he tells of "sick feelings" and his struggle to give up the habit. He was a very serious man where his work was concerned, hating to waste a day, absorbed in playwrighting and the theatre. In another, more formal diary, he records the creation of plays, rehearsals, family birthdays and anniversaries. He destroyed the scribbling diaries from time to time. If these diaries had survived, what a picture of the great dramatist would have remained but he did not want his inner revelations made public, unlike many "secret" diarists who really write for future readers. The 1925 scribbling diary is the only one to survive and we have Agnes to thank for that as she hid it and in the stormy times ahead she refused to give it up. She was reviled for this and nastily accused of stealing it. It is now in the Yale archives and published by the Yale Press. (Lett still puts out diaries in London some even with gilt edged pages, leather bound, with ribbon markers.)

In O'Neill's cottage on winter nights, the cedar logs burning in the fireplace, the dog Finn Mac Cool stretched out on the mat, the playwright could "suffer his Promethean Torments and Dionysian ecstasies". The sound of the surf below pounding against the cliffs was the accompaniment to his searching into the souls of men whose actions produced the human essence of his plays. In spite of honours and acknowledgment as a great dramatist, this so-called Broadway Elizabethan was shaken with doubts and torments. That January of 1925 he drank long and deep. The drafts from the winter storms blowing along the coast, soughing through the trees, would swirl the tobacco smoke and alcoholic fumes around the room, mixing with the aromatic scent of burning cedar wood.

Finn's Irish heart ached for his adored master. From his own ancestral depths he knew about the demons of the spirit world that drove the great geniuses of Ireland. When he dreamed of the lights dancing on misty bogs and "the little people" half seen in the heather he yelped and twitched in his sleep.

"The days are silly dreams — no swim to-day," O'Neill wrote. It was a hard struggle. "Cutting down a bit but still too miserably disorganised to really make it." He was cutting down on smoking as well as drinking and soon started to feel less "depressed and shaky". He stopped drinking except for ale with meals. He greatly enjoyed the English ale and German beer available on the island. After two days of "cutting down" he managed to give up smoking. All this would not be forever but the sun, swimming, climbing up and down the cliff wrought wonderful changes for the better in his health. His mind was also revitalized. He wrote one of his most successful plays, *The Great God Brown,* in the next two months.

In island life there are always visitors, and the O'Neills were not long settled in Campsea when one afternoon while they were taking a walk along the beach they met Mrs. Charlotte "Tottie" Barbour. She was associated with the Provincetown Players, who had produced O'Neill's early plays. She was accompanied by a fair-haired younger sister, Alice, who loved the sun and swam strongly. "Sister a Peach!" recorded O'Neill. "Athletic swimmer's figure — out-of-door girl - simple (perhaps too) and unspoiled." The women were staying at the Elbow Beach Hotel where pleasant walks would bring them to Campsea along the shore.

Alice became O'Neill's swimming companion. He swam long distances every day until his strength, building up, allowed him to do one-third of a mile from Campsea down to Elbow. His strokes were the crawl and what he called the breast crawl. He and Alice swam in tandem, keeping pace in the translucent surf just beyond the breaking of the waves that rolled in toward the shore. There is no doubt this angel of mercy played a part in restoring O'Neill to health and vigour. Sometimes he would go into the hotel with Alice or bring her home for lunch. Agnes, in an advanced stage of pregnancy, did not view the slim Alice without distress. The O'Neills had various fights over her. "Agnes very sore. Fight. Stabbed screen," he wrote. However, he climbed down the cliff with his wife in the afternoon to have a swim. "Walk with her at night in moonlight with Finn", he added.

O'Neill occasionally burst forth in romantic poetry, but no prize was ever forthcoming for these writings. He wrote a poem at this time to Alice. It was heady for him to have a youthful admirer for a swimming companion. Mrs. Barbour and Alice often went to Campsea for tea for the O'Neills had adopted this English habit. They all went out dining together in the evenings. He was no dancer and lied his way out of taking the ladies dancing. Once he could not get out of it: "In eve was forced to go to dance at Elbow Beach Hotel with Mrs Bisch & Agnes. A great bore! Met many dull folk. Danced once with Mrs. B—in crepe-rubber soles!" He was deeply involved in writing *The Great God Brown* but found the inspiration to compose this poem to Alice:

TO ALICE

The sun
And you
Two things in life
Are true

Two things are true
You are one
Your hair
And the sun.

Your eyes
And the sea
Innocence
And liberty.

Rusty chains
Ease the soul
We are wise
But you are whole.

You, the sun and sea,
Trinity!
Sweet spirit, pass on
Keep the dream
Beauty
Into infinity.

Agnes' jealousy subsided somewhat, as she knew in her heart O'Neill was not in love with the girl, although they still got into fights over her. They all continued to go about together and one evening drove into Hamilton to dine at the New Windsor to enjoy the local scallops. At the time the bays and coves of Bermuda abounded in large tender scallops, the shells sometimes measuring four to five inches across. They were a great delicacy, always served on the half-shell. They sold in the market for thirty cents the dozen. There are none today because they have been completely fished out. (At the present time, the Bermuda Biological Station, which is affiliated with the famous marine institute in Woods Hole, Massachusetts, has a programme in hand of breeding scallops in the hope they will grow again in the sandy bays.)

Agnes coped with the domestic side of Campsea, really a summer-camp-style place, with a leaky roof. From the valley behind the house, a farmer brought fresh milk daily, eggs from the chickens that scratched around his yard, and newly gathered vegetables from his fields. For other supplies Agnes removed the receiver from the big wooden telephone on the wall and, if no one was talking on the party line, she wound the handle to attract the operator and asked for the grocery store in Hamilton. Eventually a horse and cart would arrive with the order. If she wanted fish they would listen for the sound of the conch shell announcing the approach of a horse and cart with fresh fish, snappers, rockfish, yellowtails and crayfish. Someone would dash down the hill and intercept the cart.

Occasionally, early in the morning if the wind was northerly, the squeals of a terrified pig being butchered in the valley below rose to shatter the air. Shivers ran through the household to hear the plight of the poor beast. Later in the day the farmer would bring up a pale pink cut of fresh pork with the crackling on it. Bermudian cooks liked to stuff the joint and roast it in the oven on top of the kerosene stove. They browned the newly dug potatoes around the meat, the crackling turned brown and crisp. They served it all with fresh peas, apple sauce and gravy.

The cost of living was important to the O'Neills as they never knew where they were regarding income. This was in spite of the fact that O'Neill was at the peak of his output as a writer. He would never again be as prolific as he was in the twenties when he lived partly in Bermuda. He suggested to one producer, who was frequently late in paying royalties, that authors be paid weekly, the same as actors. He did not prevail with this idea. In the spring of 1925 the insecurity he and Agnes often felt began to be alleviated when *Desire Under the Elms* reached Broadway and became a triumphant success.

Much could be bought for a pound sterling in 1925 when the pound stood at five dollars. Tourists could spend American and Canadian dollars on the island - the businessmen in Hamilton being loath to turn down money of whatever description. However, the legal and main currency was the British pound, which divided into many delightful coins. Among these were the florin, the diminutive silver threepenny bit, and the big copper penny with the sovereign's head on one side and on the other Britannia ruling the waves, holding a shield embossed with the Union Jack. Old Victorian coins were still in circulation and a shopper could receive in change a silky silver 'thruppence' with the head of Queen Victoria as a young woman, her hair swept up in a traily bun at the back. Later, after Prince Albert died, she was always portrayed in her widow's weeds. In 1920 the coinage of George V was remodelled and the silver content debased. However, for many years the old coins with the high silver content continued to circulate. Gold coins were out of circulation but the sovereign could still be bought at face value at the two Bermudian banks. A sovereign, which was worth one pound, contained approximately $1/4$ ounce of gold so with the pound at $5 an ounce of gold could be bought in coins for $20.

Agnes, the children and Gaga spent time at Campsea working out the value of their spending money. Everyday items were priced in pounds, shillings and pence: the pound divided into twenty shillings, the shillings divided into twelve pence and the pence into half pence. Written down one pound ten shillings and tuppence, ha'penny looked like: £1. .10s. .2^1/2d. The crossed capital L, the pound sign, stood for Libra with her scales of true balance, the s. for the shilling sign and the d. for a penny derived from the Latin *denarius* taken from an ancient Roman silver coin denoting the value of ten asses! When Shane went to school he had to do sums of division, multiplication and subtraction in this tortuous currency.

O'Neill continued with the huge task of writing *The Great God Brown*, which among all his plays would always be for him a special favourite. In his working diary for the whole month of February is one simple entry denoting the days spent writing:

FEBRUARY
1-28
"The Great God Brown"

Not a day off! He was completely absorbed in the creation of the play. On a cold, cloudy day he entered, "Labored on 'B'. This scene a hard one" Another entry reads, "Strove again with the last scene, Act III — Won't come right." He used Agnes as a sounding board by reading some of the play to her one evening. He entered in his diary "read some excerpts of 'B' to Agnes who seemed much moved by them."

In this drama, the players wear masks, as was the style in the ancient Greek theatre. The mask was held by the actor in front of his face symbolising the face he presents to the world while his asides spoken to the audience reveal his true personality. The story tells of the extremes of the artistic temperament of Dion, confronted by the hard practicality of the business world, epitomised by Billy Brown. The undying love of Margaret for Dion is incomprehensible to Brown, who wants her for himself. How, wonders Billy, could Margaret lavish her love on the slightly mad, dissolute Dion and marry him, when he, Billy, could have given her his steady love, security, and a life of ease? Working in Brown's architectural establishment, Dion creates a master-piece of a design for an important building. Dion dies in poverty and distress but his design will be used and his name will be remembered. Brown, who is so important in life, in death will be forgotten.

A Bermudian in love with the theatre was Henry Wilkinson. He was the doctor of public health in Bermuda, a man of precise mind and quiet humour. He was an historian and had published several books on the history of Bermuda. He spent his holidays in New York or London where his chief enjoyment was the theatre. O'Neill liked his company and welcomed his visits. Henry Wilkinson was at Campsea in the evening of the day O'Neill finished *The Great God Brown*. He found the dramatist nervous and exhausted, although exhilarated in part. The tremendous effort of the past weeks and the deep emotional involve-ment with the characters had made O'Neill write in his diary "finished in tears - couldn't help myself".

A great fan of Bermuda and a frequent visitor was James Thurber, whose ticklish humour O'Neill did not escape. He writes, "Everything from chagrin to humiliation has happened to me in the long years of my going to see Eugene O'Neill's plays". He goes on with anecdotes, one of which relates how he took his uncle to see *The Hairy Ape*. The uncle took exception to something Yank said and he tried to climb over the footlights to straighten the actor out. Thurber also got off some witticisms on O'Neill's use of masks and asides causing an actor to become two people, as he put it, or two actors to become one man and ends, "There is, as the saying goes, no use in crying over split person-alities". James Thurber loved Bermuda and the family came for many years. He became friends with the editor of the *Bermudian* magazine, even contributing articles and drawings to the publication.

While O'Neill had been suffering the throes of creative playwriting in that winter of 1925, Agnes was writing a play of her own. When she and O'Neill met in Greenwich Village, she was supporting herself by writing and continued her career after they were married. She wrote short stories, some very successful, and novelettes for pulp magazines. Her father was a painter of some distinction and she had been sent to art school, but later decided that she would rather become a writer. O'Neill records in his diary: "Tried to work on A's *Guilty One* to-day—read three acts—but no interest. Last 2 acts very bad—need restructuring". Some inner compulsion seemed to drive Agnes to attempt to rival O'Neill, rather than stick to fiction where her talent lay. She had chosen an insuperable task and not one likely to make either herself or husband happy.

Three months from her due date, Agnes could not ride a bicycle over the rough coral roads. Gangs of convicts could be seen by the side of the roads cracking the hard coral into "jail nuts". These were compressed by steamrollers to make the surface of the roads. Heavy rain and wheels eroded this surface leaving it uneven and bumpy. Down the hill from Campsea the South Shore Road led into town about four miles away. A horse-drawn bus came along several times a day and in the afternoon when the O'Neills wanted to go to Hamilton they took the bus.

The *Somerset Express* provided passenger and freight service between Hamilton and Somerset for seventy years. (*Bermudian Magazine*)

Agnes would have to be helped up the two steps of this bus where she could sit on the wooden bench. Parcels were piled on top of the bus for delivery at various stops; sometimes a few puzzled chickens travelled up there grumbling in a crate as the bus rumbled along the uneven road. For Shane and Barbara it was a great treat. At every stop were expectant people waiting to receive something from the driver or to give something to be delivered further along. Some people got off and others boarded. If a sudden squall came up side curtains were hastily rolled down to ward off the rain. It became damp and steamy in the dimmed light of the bus, the odours pungent.

The bus could be a social meeting place too, as O'Neill recorded after shopping in Hamilton, "Bought sweaters and ties — met Harvard fellow and a poet-playwright — also Wilbur Jenkins' mother from New London coming back on bus".

The children loved the bus and loved to wander about the town with Gaga. They could buy a penny's worth of licorice sweets called "black babies" as they were stamped out in the form of infants. Marbles were popular with local children who played complicated games with them. For a few pennies Shane could buy a wooden top, wind the string round and then dash it to the ground by whipping the string away. The top would spin, dance and rush here and there while the children would jump to get out of its way. Boys fashioned bows and arrows out of oleander or canes, only having to buy tuppence worth of string. O'Neill recorded in his diary how he made a bow and arrow for Shane.

In town O'Neill stopped at the library, had his hair cut, or shopped. He had no sartorial ambitions in those days and was chiefly interested in sweaters but ordered a suit to be made in London. He bought a polo coat and a raglan-sleeve Irish tweed topcoat. Goods in the shops were mostly Scottish woollens and fine china and crystal from England. Bermudian men wore the traditional shorts even at night—black shorts, black knee socks, black tie and dinner jacket! Women never wore shorts or trousers even for golf and tennis.

O'Neill had brought his dinner jacket with him and he records he put on "soup and fish" (a joking name for a tuxedo implying an important dinner where soup _and_ fish would precede the main course) when he went to St. George's, at the East End, for dinner and to watch the female Olympic swimmers who were visiting the island. Mrs. Barbour and Alice shared a hired carriage with Agnes and O'Neill for the hour and a half drive to the old capital of Bermuda, settled in the seventeenth century. Along the narrow streets were quaint old houses built of stone in the unique architectural style of the island. The stocks still stood in the square where malefactors used to be secured in the yoke by neck and arms making them the objects of ridicule and targets of rotten eggs. Forts lay to the east along the cliffs ready to repel any piratical marauders from the sea. The British garrison was stationed nearby.

The St. George Hotel overlooked the town and the driver had to urge his horses to pull the heavy carriage to the top of the hill. He then slowed into the line of equipages and hacks dropping off their passengers at the front door. Grooms spent the evening at the hotel stables where they took the horses out of the shafts to rest for the return journey. The woollen Scottish tartan rugs were refolded and placed on the seats. The candles in the lamps were snuffed. The drivers passed the evening together with a spot of rum and a game of dice or cards.

The hotel was proud of its indoor swimming pool, built in 1922, the only one on the island. The locker rooms were set back surrounding the pool and above was a balcony for viewing the swimming and diving events. The boxes for important visitors were at one end and after dinner O'Neill was gratified to find his was next to the Governor's. "Some swank", he recorded.

Musicians were on hand and when His Excellency and party arrived all stood and "God Save the King" rang out. The Furness Withy Steamship Company, which served the island, brought the young Olympians on a free trip to Bermuda. O'Neill noted their names in his diary: Ederle, Riggin and Wainwright. It was Gertrude Ederle, still in her teens, who had recently swum the English Channel, the first woman to do so. The girls excelled in the backstroke and free style swimming.

O'Neill was now a hardy and strong swimmer not daunted by 60 degree temperatures, always trying to improve his strokes and rhythm. He marked out distances along the beach. He kept records of his daily progress. He wanted to watch the young swimmers to see how the best in the world swam. He wrote: "...everybody at hotel very subservient" and that he had a "nice ride". However, he was disappointed in the girls; "Typical gum-chewing Coney Islanders with thighs like elephant's heinie".

At Easter the Trotts came to their holiday cottage amongst the cedars. Along the lane came a procession of a carriage, carts and bicycles, bringing the large family of three boys and two girls. The O'Neills were astonished to see a cow arriving tethered in a trolley cart. Mrs Trott, later Lady Trott when her husband was knighted by the King, would not move without her well cared for cow as milk could carry various diseases.

A South Shore beach. *(Bermuda Archives)*

There was only one path down the steep cliff to the beach and as the Trotts filed along past the O'Neill cottages they would meet O'Neill himself, sometimes, setting out for his swim. Margaret then aged twelve reflects "He was never friendly or humorous but always kind. I doubt if anyone ever really knew him. His dark eyes and cadaverous face created a feeling of tragedy." Little blonde Polly who was younger remembers how tall and thin he was. "He was attractive," she says, "with wonderful eyes." Margaret added, "When we got to the beach he would swim off a great distance."

At home at Campsea, special days were when the eagerly awaited mail arrived from the United States. It was brought twice weekly by the ships plying from New York. They arrived early in the morning so the mail reached the Paget Post Office, by horse-drawn van, in the afternoon. Sometimes O'Neill would bicycle over to pick it up as the postman might not get to his home until the following day. He looked forward to theatre news, assurance that his royalties had been paid and relished the arrival of the books he had ordered. From England ships came every two weeks with news for the English community of loved ones and business. From whatever direction they came, the newspapers and magazines the ships brought flew off the stands in Hamilton.

Once in 1925 the airship *Los Angeles* arrived bringing the first airmail to Bermuda. Later on the same day the great dirigible rose in the sky carrying the return mail. This experimental airmail flight did not occur again. Regular airmail was ten years away, when the flying boats of British Overseas Airways and Pan American would provide regular service in the late 1930s.

The dirigible *Los Angeles* moored to its parent ship *Patoka*, anchored in Grassy Bay after bringing the first airmail to Bermuda. *(Bermudian Magazine)*

O'Neill was a formidable correspondent and it is fortunate that a huge number of his letters have survived. They reveal so many sides of his dynamic personality, from his "somber profundity" to his seldom seen impish humour. He lived in an era when letter writing was a way of life; it was the only way to communicate with distant family, friends and business associates. In Bermuda brief overseas messages could be sent and received by cable. The long distance telephone was a thing of the future.

The excitement in the O'Neill household centred around the mail telling of the wild news about *Desire Under the Elms*. The New York District Attorney, Joab Banton, threatened to close the drama down when it arrived on Broadway from the Greenwich Village Theatre. In the play many human crimes take place. While these wicked, sexy deeds can be easily read about even in the Bible, there they can be hushed between the sacred pages. To see them acted out on the stage was too much for the American general public. The permissive age had not dawned and the puritanical keepers of public morals were affronted. Uptown the play was coining money.

O'Neill certainly needed the money, but was dismayed by the reason the play drew such big audiences. He regarded the drama as a serious tragedy. He wrote angrily, "the low minded, looking for smut, they are highly disappointed or else laugh whenever they imagine double meanings". The ships brought the newspapers and a cable informed him that 13,500 people saw *Desire* in one week. "Helped by scandal, damn it!" he wrote. Later, when he heard there would be no indictment he vented his feelings: "Old Banton seems to be beaten again, the bloody ass!" The play has been called the great American domestic horror story.

O'Neill wrote enthusiastically about Bermuda to an old friend, the drama critic Jean Nathan, "The climate is grand, there is absolutely nothing to do, and the German bottled beer and the English bottled ale are both excellent. It has proved a profitable winter for me. I've gotten more work done than in the corresponding seasons up north in many years. The frost and hard cider of too many successive New England winters are slowly being rendered out of my system". To Macgowan, he wrote, "You simply must come down! It's grand here!"

Just then, coming down to stay was Eugene Jr., aged 14, O'Neill's son by a previous marriage. The boy lived with his mother and step-father and did not often see O'Neill, who was nevertheless fond of him. In 1909 O'Neill met and courted Kathleen Jenkins, a young woman of respectable family, whose parents disapproved of their daughter's suitor. O'Neill's father, James, was opposed to his son entertaining any serious thoughts toward marriage. A more unsuitable candidate for a husband than the twenty year old O'Neill, in those days, could scarcely be imagined. He was just back from his voyages before the mast and in old tramp ships, during which he had developed a taste for waterfront taverns and the company of seafarers. His father, to put distance between him and Kathleen, persuaded him to go on a gold prospecting expedition which was setting out for Honduras. The young couple was secretly married just before O'Neill left. Kathleen was pregnant.

Although he wrote to his mother from Honduras that he was certain there would be "lots of gold further up the river in the mountains", he never found any. A serious bout of malaria decided him to return to New York. Unbelievably he did not rejoin Kathleen, nor did he see the son she had born him, Eugene Junior. Her parents were scandalised and when all hope of their daughter's marriage was gone they arranged a divorce. When the boy was five years old Kathleen married George Pitt-Smith.

In Bermuda at the end of March, in the beautiful spring weather, O'Neill, his play finished, records, "Carriage early and met Eugene (Junior)" who had made the journey from New York by himself. Regrettably, O'Neill was back on his old habit during Eugene's visit, but spent much time on the beach with his sons. To interest boys, at the top of the cliff where the path starts to descend to the beach is a seventeenth century gun emplacement where a cannon lay sleeping in the grasses and wild flowers, the gun carriage long since rotted away. In the ammunition chambers land crabs made their burrows. A more recent fortification, built in the eighteen hundreds, was overgrown and eroded by wind and rain. The forts were built in an area of coastal defense. The early settlers feared the approach of Spaniards, French or pirates in the deep water beyond the reef, not far from the shore. It would have been easy for an invading force to lower boats and land on the beach below.

One afternoon his father took Eugene to Hamilton to show him the colonial capital and to buy him some clothes. (O'Neill was not without conscience towards him for when Kathleen had asked for help with his education, he had readily agreed.) O'Neill tried to be a pal to the children, but he never succeeded and once remarked he did not know what to say to them.

The highlight of the visit was when his father hired a sailing boat to take a party to an island off Somerset at the West End. The captain sailed past the lugubrious spot where the body of a murdered woman had been raised from the bottom. Her husband, a man called Skeeters, had killed his wife in a rage and put the body in an old trunk which he slipped overboard from his fishing boat. The solution to the mystery of her disappearance came a few weeks later when oil from her body glimmering on the surface of the sea led to its discovery.

Southcote   JBW

Chapter 3

"It's a goil!" Oona O'Neill born on May 14th, 1925 at Southcote.
The playwright in creative doldrums – battling alcoholism.

Agnes decided not to go to the King Edward VII Memorial Hospital, but
to have the baby at home. It was still common practice for babies to be
born at home as maternity was considered a natural process and
nothing to make a fuss over. Sometimes only a midwife attended the
mother. It was agreed that as Campsea was nothing more than a
wooden bungalow with a leaky roof, the O'Neills would find a more
suitable house. They rented a large place called Southcote, built of coral
stone, and standing in extensive grounds. It was not far away from
Campsea and had access to the same beach. Mrs. Bish, a friend and
trained nurse, was staying in Bermuda with her children and would
look after Agnes. She was the wife of Dr. Louis Bish, a New York
psychiatrist to whom O'Neill would later turn for help with his drinking problem.

O'Neill and Agnes stole away from Campsea and spent the first
night in their new home, Southcote, by themselves. The rest of the
family would move in the next day. It was their seventh wedding
anniversary and he was disappointed the Chinese shawl he had ordered for Agnes had not arrived in time. The large popular shawls were
much in fashion, made of heavy silk embroidered with coloured
flowers. They had long fringes. When draped about the figure a shawl
would hang gracefully to well below the waist. Fringes were "in" and

the flappers really got them jiggling while dancing the Charleston. Agnes wanted one and looked forward to wearing it when svelte again. Meanwhile it could drape her figure, which was so large that O'Neill thought they might have twins.

Although she was in the last stages of pregnancy, Agnes welcomed Jimmy Light to stay, an old friend of O'Neill's who had acted in his early plays. He came down with socialites Felton and Sara Elkins, who stayed nearby at the South Shore Hotel. Elkins was a millionaire playboy who fancied himself as a dramatist and was an old drinking pal of O'Neill's. After the emotional experience and day-to-day toil of *The Great God Brown*, it was a release for him to have his light-hearted friends arrive. He fell off the wagon, talked theatre, went picnicking and swimming and showed them the island.

The O'Neills new landlords at Southcote were the Smiths. Agnes suffered Bermudian effrontery because they had moved into Southcote without signing the lease—an illegality. One morning an old maiden lady, called Aunt Lilla Smith, came round with the lease form. These forms were popular because they were easily drawn up, thus sidestepping the necessity for a lawyer. She was greeted by Agnes, dressed in capacious loose garments, a vibrant young woman of thirty-two with a big smile, who informed Aunt Lilla her husband was asleep and could not be disturbed. Aunt Lilla beat a retreat, returning the following afternoon only to be told again that O'Neill was asleep. When she expressed her annoyance Agnes said, "You don't seem to realise who my husband is". "I don't care who he is," was the retort, "I shall be back in the morning and if he doesn't sign you can all get out." Later, one of the Smiths saw *Desire Under the Elms* and said if they had known what sort of plays O'Neill wrote they would never have rented them the house! As to the lease, Agnes protected O'Neill from petty annoyances and finally she and Aunt Lilla decided the matter amicably. Agnes signed the lease.

Agnes was to have the baby at home, attended by Dr. W.E. Tucker, who came along to see her on his rounds in his horse drawn trap. A.A. Milne had just taken the nursery world by storm with his book, *When We Were Very Young*. The doctor loved the small characters who inhabited Milne's world and spared time to recite his favourite to little Shane, "James James Morrison Morrison". Dr. Tucker had been a rugger blue at Cambridge and while he was an intern at St. George's Hospital in London, had captained the famous rugby team Blackheath.

He was a congenial, capable, and energetic medical man. O'Neill liked him and would accompany him on his house visits, often driving long distances. Sometimes they would drive at night, the rain warded off by a long black waterproof sheet drawn across the lurching buggy at eye level. The horse, ears back, splashed through the puddles, the candles spluttered in the carriage lamps and rooster tails of mud flew off the wheels.

The burly doctor had kindly blue eyes, fair hair, graying then, and a nose somewhat out of joint - a souvenir of the playing fields of England. He coped actively and daily with physical disaster and mental collapse. The wiry O'Neill, with large intense dark eyes, black brows and hair, introspective in nature, was in great contrast to his companion. He diagnosed and treated with his mighty pen other kinds of human ills.

The doctor's and writer's conversation blew away over the oleander hedges into the sage bushes, lost to posterity. To Sister Mary Leo, O'Neill wrote from Bermuda, "I write of the spiritually and physically disinherited... I write tragedy. Tragedy is what it is. It is only those who are ignoble in themselves who cannot appreciate the nobility of tragedy."

As the time grew near for the birth of his child, O'Neill wrote in a letter, "our twin girls are expected any moment now – but then ladies always make you wait, don't they – but it is getting on my nerves while Agnes is as calm as calm – couvade, is that what they call it?" He refers to a primitive custom in which the expectant father took to his bed as if he were giving birth to the child. On the fourteenth of May the baby, a girl, arrived safely. O'Neill wired Macgowan "It's a goil. Allah be merciful. According to indications will be first lady announcer at Polo Grounds. Predict great future grand opera. Agnes and baby all serene." The name Oona was chosen, which means Agnes in Irish.

The O'Neills were spending about two and half months at Southcote after the birth of Oona before leaving for the United States. The beautiful spring weather continued, the oleanders in bloom. The air was scented with flowers and the soft briny smell of the sea. The beach was a short walk from the house down the Tribe Road. These straight narrow roads crossed the island at intervals giving public access to the water. Miss Edith Smith, now in her nineties and still living near Southcote, remembers seeing the O'Neills often with friends and dogs lunching on the pink sands. O'Neill was back on his old bad habit - he records feeling "very shaky and nervous". No creative winds fanned his genius; he seemed becalmed in a baffling doldrum.

The dogs Finn and Bowser chased around the sloping lawns through the Surinam cherry groves barking at any strangers. Physical violence in Bermuda was rare but there were peeping toms and the occasional sneak thief. The dogs took care to guard Southcote from intruders. An exhibitionist had exposed himself to the Bish children's nurse on the beach. The habit of "exposing" was not uncommon and a "flash" could even occur in Hamilton in broad daylight. If at night, the "exposure" would be well illuminated by flashlight! O'Neill decided to report the beach incident to the police. "Scotch Bobby came over", he records. To be on the safe side he rode into Hamilton on his "wheel" (Bermudian for bicycle which he had adopted) and in American style bought a gun and bullets. The police in Bermuda, mostly Englishmen, were unarmed, as they are to this day in the British tradition.

At night in the parish Finn was heard baying the moon. The press took a swipe at O'Neill in their column "They Say"...

> That the famous playwright Eugene O'Neill who is staying here is meeting with great success with his remarkable plays.
> That it will be interesting to see the one he is writing here.
> That if he could put his dog in it would be a howling success.

The outside world came to Bermuda through radio programmes from New York, which the authorities hoped would be a great boon to education in the island. O'Neill's *Bound East for Cardiff* was heard that winter over the wireless. Another broadcast from America was given by Mrs. Bish's husband Dr. Louis Bish, on the "Psychology of Playwrighting". They went in to Hamilton to listen, as the O'Neills had no radio, and they were very disappointed with the heavy static. O'Neill records, "Nothing but noise with only the words Eugene O'Neill distinguishable".

He was pleased to meet Dr. Bish when he arrived in the island in May. He liked him and would later seek the doctor's help professionally when the family returned to New York, for O'Neill was becoming convinced that before long he would have to choose between his work and his drinking.

In May O'Neill was too downcast to make notes on his reading. In the evenings he had read Freud's *Group Psychology and Beyond the*

Finn Mac Cool with his Irish-American master at Campsea. *(Louis Shaeffer)*

Pleasure Principle. Ever interested in ancient Greek drama, he read Walter Pater's *Greek Portraits and Greek Studies.* Of Nietzsche's *Birth of Tragedy* he wrote, "Most stimulating book on drama ever written." He also enjoyed Aldous Huxley's *Antic Hay.*

One day when the dramatist was making his accustomed look-in at the Bermuda Book Store in Hamilton, he was surprised to be offered James Joyce's *Ulysses,* surreptitiously taken out from under the counter. At that time the book was banned in England and the United States. The big paperback had been printed in France where American travellers bought it and brought it back home concealed in their luggage. The

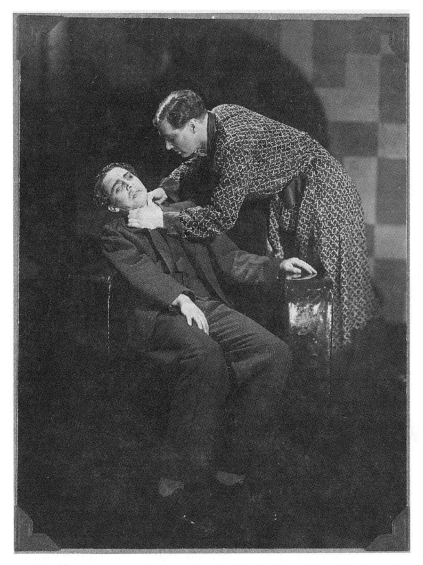

In the *Great God Brown*, Brown grabs Dion by the throat. The play "remains in the end a fascinating, half-mad enigma". (*Yale University*).

"seminal book" is said to have influenced O'Neill's method of writing *Strange Interlude*.

Staying in the "Isle of Devils" it was natural for O'Neill to read *The Tempest*. William Shakespeare had been inspired by the story circulating in London of the wreck of the *Sea Venture* and the raging tempest which had also carried away the rest of Admiral Somers' fleet. In his play the great bard refers to the "still vexed Bermoothes". O'Neill enters no comments in his diary after reading *The Tempest*. A fanciful writer has drawn a comparison between the pure and simple Miranda, Prospero's daughter and O'Neill's swimming companion, the "sweet spirit" Alice.

O'Neill's despondency was relieved by visitors. He got up early one fine May morning to go into Hamilton to meet his friends on board the boat that docked at nine. He joined the throng on the wharf; people were there to meet passengers and idlers were there to watch the show. He was delighted to pick out his old friends, Kenneth Macgowan and Robert Edmund Jones, waving to him from the deck rail. The ship tooted, speaking to the tugs warping it around in the narrow harbour. The great ropes were dragged up onto the wharf and placed around the bollards. The rat baffles were attached to prevent the creatures from walking up the ropes and boarding the ship.

O'Neill led his friends away into the street full of carts and carriages, bicycles and pedestrians and found a horse-drawn surrey with a fringe on top to take them to Southcote. Both men had been associated with him in the theatre since his early plays. They had also been involved in the management of the Greenwich Village Theatre and the early days of the Theatre Guild in New York. O'Neill was anxious to show them *The Great God Brown*, which he considered "the ceiling" of his literary attainment. On the evening of their arrival he read them the first part of the play. "Both much impressed," he recorded.

Agnes was welcoming as usual to her husband's friends but she felt some anxiety. He had been on the wagon for six days before they arrived and she hoped he would manage to continue on it. They talked constant theatre, bringing the dramatist up to date on the latest activities in New York. While in Bermuda he had written to Macgowan frequently, promoting his plays, thinking about who would put up the money, suggesting suitable actors and actresses for the parts and, in general, considering the production and management of scenery. He needed the income from his writing, whether new productions, revivals or publications of plays and poems. He depended on his two friends and he wanted them to enjoy their holiday. They took lunch to the beach, sunned themselves, played tennis and went sailing.

When the family were ready to leave Bermuda at the end of June, O'Neill had not had a drink for twenty-nine days. He was deeply tanned, improved in health, handsome and distinguished, but for all his physical toughness he had a diffident air and the thoughtfulness in his dark eyes betrayed the intellectual. The ocean was calm even as the *Fort St. George* crossed the Gulf Stream on their voyage north. They had fine staterooms and little Oona, now two months old, was unperturbed by life on shipboard, he recorded in his diary. O'Neill was glad to see Macgowan and his agent Richard Madden on the pier to meet him. He took the family over to settle into the Lafayette Hotel and in the afternoon he went to Dr. Bish for treatment.

The O'Neills had taken a house in Nantucket for the summer months and after a few days in the city Agnes moved there with the children, leaving her husband to finish his business. He wrote theatre news to Agnes from New York and about his visit to David Belasco who had produced a play in 1879 in which O'Neill's father, James, had starred. "He certainly admires *Marco*, God bless him! He showed us over his place - a truly amazing museum and packed with wonderful stuff he collected." John Barrymore had wired that he looked forward to reading the script. O'Neill liked Walter Huston more every time he saw him and wanted to try him in a part in *The Fountain*. He ended, "I'm Damn Lonely! Every second I spend alone in the room I miss you like the devil - and I miss Oona over on the couch. I really love her! Never thought I could a baby! And I love you my dear wife and pal, more than I have power to say! When you leave me I really feel a sensation of having had some vital part of me removed. My heart, probably - it's with you in Nantucket! Good night darling! My love to Shane and Oona and kisses for all of you! Gene"

O'Neill had been a friend and admirer of the actor and singer Paul Robeson for many years. Robeson had played the lead part of Jim Harris in *All God's Chillun Got Wings*. The following September, Robeson was scheduled to play the title role in *Emperor Jones* in London. One evening after Agnes left for Nantucket, O'Neill went with Robeson to Harlem where the jazz and the shows were very much in vogue. The playwright had not been drinking for forty-eight days, but the all night spree prompted him to go on a tremendous bender which lasted for days. "Disaster", he entered. He went out to spend a few days with the Macgowans in the country to rest. Before going to Nantucket to join his family he saw Dr. Louis Bish who prescribed verinol, a commonly prescribed sleeping drug in those days.

O'Neill took the boat to Nantucket at the end of July and was disappointed to find the house he had rented not to his liking, right on

the road and lacking privacy. Always temperamental about his sur-
roundings, he passed August with no work done, but his drinking was
under control and remained so. Good news came by cable from London
saying *The Emperor Jones*, which had opened at the Ambassadors
Theatre, was a big hit. He started work on a new play, *Lazarus Laughed*.
He cut down smoking and swam through into October in the cold water
off Nantucket.

The family moved to their home, Brook Farm, in Connecticut for the
autumn and O'Neill was often in New York for the production of *The
Fountain*. He was enjoying being a celebrity in the city. At home, Agnes
welcomed their many friends who came out to visit, including Mrs.
Tottie Barbour and Alice. When he was at home with the family O'Neill
interspersed his sporadic writing with working in the woods, trimming
trees and chopping wood. The autumn days drew in and in the woods
the leafless trees had begun their winter sleep. The evenings were long
and dark, the fire in the hearth, the curtains drawn against the New
England countryside, wintry and bleak. By November he was planning
the scenes for *Lazarus* and records his creative days when he started the
dialogue but the terrible battle with drinking overcame him and work
dwindled away. He tried to get over feeling "mentally disorganised".
At home he was bored: "R field is no home for me! Dull as hell". Before
Christmas, in spite of exercise, he was "sick plus melancholia with a
capital M".

O'Neill's friends, Kenneth Macgowan and Jimmy Light, who were
trying to cast *The Great God Brown*, scheduled to open in January, made
the cold journey out from New York to see him. Macgowan, greatly
concerned about O'Neill, had made an appointment for him to see Dr.
Gilbert A. Hamilton, a prominent psychiatrist. "A ray of hope amid
general sick despair", wrote O'Neill. He cut down drinking. "Nerves
all shot to hell". "Have to go down to Brown rehearsals soon. *Must* get
in shape." On New Year's day he was on the wagon "Good'bye—
without regret— 1925 (except for a few months in Bermuda)".

On New Year's Day he hailed "Welcome to a new dawn, I pray!" The
events of the year to come would change his whole life. In his working
diary he wrote "New era begins", not knowing how true a prediction
he was making.

Bellevue

Chapter 4

The family returns in the spring and rents Bellevue.
The playwright, invigorated, completes the play *Lazarus Laughed*.

In the winter of 1926, the departure for Bermuda was delayed by the rehearsals of *The Great God Brown*, written the year before at Campsea. O'Neill hoped this unusual play, with the innovation of masks worn by the actors in the Greek tradition, would be well received by the public. The year was starting well for him with other plays in production.

Theatregoers in Philadelphia packed the house to see *Desire Under the Elms* and to discover the scandalous ends to which the farming New England Cabots were driven by their desires. In London, audiences pressed to see Robeson experience the hallucinations of the black Emperor Jones being hunted at night in the moonlit tropical forest, threatened by specious animals and the spectres of his past. *The Emperor Jones* was inspired by O'Neill's West Indian travels and the black man Henri Christophe, a slave, who seized power from the French colonists and proclaimed himself Emperor of Haiti.

O'Neill was morose when he thought some people went to see his plays for reasons other than to hear their noble tragic messages but was nevertheless relieved by the financial results. It was only recently that he and Agnes had enjoyed a substantial income of over $20,000 a year. O'Neill knew only too well the gnawing anxiety of poverty. In his early twenties he had been desperately poor, right down to the change in his shabby pocket. He was no George Orwell who left us the vivid description of the slimy floor in the scullery where he washed dishes in a Paris hotel. The slimy waterfront of Buenos Aires where O'Neill was "down and out" can only be imagined. Cheap liquor and wretched food undermined his health while he lived in flop houses or slept on wharf-side benches. He waited for weeks in the Argentine in fear and suspense wondering if he would ever find a ship willing to sign him on for a passage home.

Bellevue on the South Road in Paget. (*Bermudian Magazine*)

In February 1926, as he stepped over the threshold of Bellevue in Bermuda, his poverty was long behind him. The old house, which the O'Neills had rented for the season, was one of the island's finest. From the columned porch was a view of sweeping acres and the blue sea. The property sloped down past fruit trees and planting fields to a private beach. O'Neill wanted Macgowan to see it all and wrote, "You simply must come down! Must! We have a real peach of a house this time and lots of room—beautiful grounds—private beach—all at the big bargain of 150 per. It's really the nicest house I've ever seen here-or almost anywhere else-beautifully arranged as to rooms, furnished mid-Vic. somewhat but comfortable withal, upper and lower porches, etc.-used to be one of the show places of the island they say ... Why don't you resolve to make it ... It would be worth it." O'Neill continued, "Swimming every day. Much exercise. I've gained almost six pounds in less than two weeks. Feel reborn. I was pretty low as to vitality by the time I sailed. " The year before O'Neill mentioned in his diary how the secretary he had hired did not turn up or came late, so to avoid aggravation Agnes' sister Margery, known as Budgie, was part of the household and did O'Neill's typing. He continued to Macgowan, "Budgie has accumulated the measles! Must have picked them up on the steamer, somehow. Only possible place. She has one wing of this palace as a quarantine island. Outside of which we are all fine. Same to you! Gene."

In the garden, hibiscus were in bloom and on the lawns the sweet-scented freesias bloomed amid the green grass. Redbirds nested in the grand cedars outside the windows of the old-fashioned cottage that O'Neill intended to use for writing. Inside, the ceiling was supported by cedar rafters and beams and the walls were clean with whitewash. A fireplace stood ready to warm him in the spring evenings while he read or wrote or followed his new pursuit, the study of ancient Greek. He thought it would take him four years of study before he would be able to read the Greek tragedies in the original and had the fanciful notion that knowledge of the Greek language would make a garden for his soul with a cool stream to enjoy after sweating in the heat of modern life.

He wrote to Manual Komroff, an editor at publishers Boni and Liveright, thanking him for the trouble he had taken in finding and sending down a number of books on Greek literature and philosophy. O'Neill was also studying various religions for the work he planned to do later on and asked for good translations of the Talmud and the Koran.

Down the lanes of the estate rumbled trolley carts bringing crates to the fields. Immigrant Portuguese labourers newly arrived from the Azores, working among the crops, filled the crates with potatoes, onions and Easter lilies for export to New York. The O'Neills would get used to seeing the Portuguese who spoke no English and might say a shy "bom dia". These people from the Azores sometimes brought their wives, arriving peasant poor but with honesty and integrity. Any child at the time, born on British soil was a British subject so a new race was introduced into the island and their descendants were to become leaders and professionals in the colony.

At the bottom of the hill the O'Neills, with the dogs Finn and Bowser, found their way out onto Grape Bay, named for the bay grape trees bordering the sand. Their beach spread out before them. Beyond the

The farmer harrowing his field. (*Walter Rutherford*)

breaking waves the sea was pale *eau de Nil* shading to turquoise, darkening to ultramarine on the horizon. Around the large coral rocks inshore lived many brightly coloured fish, all an interdependent part of the life of the vast coral reefs. Bermudian drivers came down there to rake up the Sargasso weed and take it away in two-wheeled box carts as fertiliser, especially for banana trees. No doubt someone warned O'Neill about the dangerous undertow; a man had been drawn under and drowned there.

O'Neill had not had time to do any writing in the first weeks of the New Year before sailing for Bermuda as he was at the theatre supervising the production of *The Great God Brown*. After the dress rehearsal he had gone home to Ridgefield avoiding the opening night, as he always did. He wrote in his diary, "Went off well by all accounts" - a modest entry considering the acclaim he received from the critics and the public. He explained Brown's character in a letter to the *New York Post*:

> Brown is the visionless demi-god of our new materialistic myth-success - building his life of exterior things - inwardly empty and resourceless, an uncreative creature of superficial preordained social grooves, a by-product forced aside into slack waters by the deep main current of life-desire.

A page of notes, written in Bermuda, about his early family relationships
that would be revealed fifteen years later in the *Long Days' Journey Into
Night*. (*Harley Hammerman*)

Materialism was on the rise everywhere and even Bermuda was not
without its "Brown". O'Neill had deep feelings for the characters in the
play created in the cottage on the windy cliff with the muffled thunder
of the surf below.

Before coming back to Bermuda that winter O'Neill made an emotionally upsetting trip to New London to settle his father's and brother's
estates. The long story of drug addiction and alcoholism of two
generations in the family, he hoped, was over. His father, at one time
a fine actor, had declined in the theatre and had turned to alcohol for

consolation. O'Neill grew up being blamed for his mother's addiction to morphine. He was born in his parents' bedroom in a hotel on Broadway where actors stayed. The hotel doctor who attended Mrs. O'Neill prescribed the narcotic for the intense pain she continued to have after childbirth. For many years she was hopelessly addicted. O'Neill's brother, James, had recently died in an institution, at the age of forty-five, a physical and mental wreck from alcohol. Somehow James' wasted life was blamed on O'Neill because of his mother's addiction. The guilt for all the family misfortunes was placed on O'Neill's shoulders. He was superstitious and his own experiences led him to believe in cursed families.

The family tragedies that would haunt him all his life receded from his mind as he refreshed himself in the peace and beauty of Bellevue. He swam every day and wrote that he felt reborn. He was not drinking. His mind was released for his play, *Lazarus Laughed*, which he had put aside since the troubled last months of 1925. It was to be an elaborate fantasy but through it would run a serious searching into man's spiritual determination to believe in, and be sure of, life after death. He wrote to Macgowan, "Lazarus" is going strong! I'm going over what I've already written in the light of many new and richer notions, chiefly connected with a working out of my mask scheme. It gains significance and depth in every way daily. I'm sitting on the tops these days. Wish I could talk over with you. Too long to wait."

The metaphysical extravaganza of *Lazarus Laughed* is set against the brutality of the Roman Empire at the time Jesus raised Lazarus from the dead. The risen Lazarus is depicted as a large vigorous man who exhorts crowds of Nazarenes and Orthodox Jews to laugh because death is overcome. "Death is dead," he laughs. Masks are used as they were in Greek drama to show emotions. Also masks show the ethnic types whom Lazarus meets on his voyage to Rome. Music, dancing and singing are interspersed. The old Roman Emperor, Tiberius, who has a twenty-year-old mistress, wishes to find out how to overcome death and regain youthfulness. He sends his son Caligula, accompanied by a Roman legion, to find Lazarus and escort him to the Imperial Palace. Once there, the young mistress falls in love with Lazarus. However, not much develops as Lazarus is not encouraging and in any case, is shortly burnt at the stake. He has failed to show Tiberius how to restore his youth and avoid death. Lazarus proclaims from the consuming flames "Death is overcome". The girl is restrained from flinging herself into the fire. The curtain falls.

While the play was being written, in the cottage nearby, Agnes was running a large household including her daughter Barbara. In the airy kitchen at Bellevue, the maids prepared the meals using the kerosene stove for most of the cooking. Once a week they got the wood-burning range going for baking the bread. The dough was kneaded, the loaves shaped up and set aside to rise covered with clean dish towels. Vents on the range were adjusted until the temperature of the oven was judged to be correct for baking.

The iceman came no more to Bellevue as he had done in the past, in his dripping ice wagon, the water sprinkling over the backyard from the melting ice. He used to come through to the pantry bringing blocks of ice held by tongs to place in the icebox. The ice gradually melted into pans placed underneath, which had to be emptied twice a day or the water would overflow on to the floor. The iceman was in the house almost daily and this led to the iceman jokes. O'Neill sent one to his friend Professor Quinn of Philadelphia. It was about a trucker who came home hot and thirsty and it went something like: As the trucker entered his home he called out "Has the iceman come?" "No" his wife called from upstairs, "but he's breathing heavily!"

The iceman, the figure of mirth, would fade into fiction now that the electric refrigerator had been invented. The glory of the pantry at Bellevue was the electric fridge, a monster up on legs with a huge motor on top. It made ice, kept food cold, never broke down and would last for twenty years.

As the beach was so far away, down through the estate, a lady tells that Agnes bought a Shetland pony called Jeff and a governess cart to take the children and the picnic baskets to the shore. It was too far to push Oona in her perambulator, especially on the return journey up the steep paths. The south shore beaches were a delight and for most of the year it was warm and sunny at lunchtime. O'Neill loved swimming and picnicking with the family after his morning's work. He wrote to his father-in-law, Edward W. Boulton: "bathing is so warm and the air so soft that you can sport around in the water on the beach in the moonlight as pleasurably as in the sunlight – Shane is in the water all the time and Oona wades about in it."

Bermuda was a healthy place for children. Childhood diseases were mild and dread epidemics of polio never occurred. The yellow fever mosquito lived in the island but there had been no cases since the turn of the century. The government took all possible steps to prevent the insect from breeding by draining stagnant water and stocking ponds with fish to eat the larvae. Around the world leprosy existed and Bermuda was no exception. The few lepers lived segregated in the leprosarium and at the time the O'Neills came, the government had just voted money to build new wooden bungalows for them. Housing for lepers was always built of wood so that when the unfortunate person died his house along with his possessions could be burnt.

Front Street in Hamilton was always a pageant and from Bellevue it was a ten-minute bicycle ride, partly downhill - a bit slower coming back. In the afternoons the O'Neills often went in to shop and some-times were invited to tea at the "yacht club", as O'Neill put it in his diary. This could have been the Royal Bermuda, a modest place in those days, upstairs in a verandahed building on Front Street, but still prestigious in international sailing. Or it could have been at the Royal Amateur Hamilton Dinghy Club, also a gathering place for the Forty Thieves (this waggish term was applied to the estimated forty well-to-do, socially prominent white families).

The water's edge on Front Street was a bustle of enterprise. Six or seven individually operated rowing boats plied to take people across the smooth water of Hamilton Harbour to the Paget shore. The rowers and passengers sat amidships, bicycles were rested across the bow and stern. This ferry service had operated on a free-enterprise basis for two hundred years. Sailing boats for hire tacked back and forth and O'Neill often rented the best, skippered by Charlie Powell. While in town O'Neill would go round the corner into Queen Street to the library situated in the beautiful garden of "Par la Ville". The Bermuda library was founded in 1830 and contained a surprising collection of fine books. Sometimes along the waterfront thoroughfare came a man ringing a huge bell crying, "Auction! Auction!" The Walkers had their auction rooms nearby where occasionally fine English silver and antique furni-ture came up for bidding.

People had to look sharp on Front Street when the cattle boat tied up alongside. Poultry, pork and veal were raised on the island but beef was another matter. Refrigerated freight was unheard of, so beef came in on the hoof. Carriages and carts were driven away from the street, merchants shut their doors, Queen Street was barricaded, the gang-plank went down and the cattle, with frightened cries, rushed ashore. Drovers with big sticks chased them along to the slaughterhouse, situated conveniently on the shore so when the cattle were killed the blood could go overboard. Big sharks lurked in the area to scavenge the fresh trimmings that were thrown into the sea.

O'Neill loved sailing and had made friends with W.B. Smith who would pick him up in his twenty-four-foot sloop, the *11th Hour,* to sail among the islands in Hamilton Harbour and the Great Sound. W.B. was a landowner from Bailey's Bay and, after investigatory trips to Europe, founded the Perfume Factory. He captured the scent of the Easter lily, the passion flower, jasmine and other local flowers. His daughter Mabs remembers sailing with O'Neill. She thought him attractive and liked him but from her then seventeen-year-old point of view, she thought him rather old.

Tea, that indispensable and genteel part of British life, was served at four o'clock throughout the colony: at Government House, in the vicarages, at tennis parties, in mansions or in cottages. Americans living on the island took up the habit and gave tea parties. O'Neill would occasionally go to one, "a pack of folks there, some new ones. A bore," he reported.

At home at Bellevue the O'Neills enjoyed the seclusion of their beach, where the only visitors were the sandpipers feeding in the rushing surf and the long-tailed tropic birds gliding over the reefs intent on fishing. Shane would run into the water, laughing to see the sandpipers skimming off over the waves. The little boy postured, ran, fell down in the sand and shouted into the wind. The dogs chased each other in the sand. Oona, holding her mother's hand, took her uncertain infant steps. As Agnes, with her daughter, paddled along the shore, she kept an eye on her husband, lean and strong far out in the sea doing a rhythmic crawl oblivious of undertow, barracudas and sharks. The sun shone; the only shadow on this family scene was cast by a fleeting cloud.

"Our home port for the next two or three years will be this here Bellevue," wrote O'Neill to Macgowan, "We are taking a lease on it at a thousand per-an enormous bargain you would agree if you saw it. Agnes and I both love the house or rather, houses! It's arranged better for our needs than any place we have ever lived in. Then again, it is not far from New York."

Regarding money he wrote, "Dear Kenneth: Just a line to catch this boat;...I beg to remind the Directors of the Greenwich Village Theatre that they are taking longer to pay royalties on "Brown" than any management I have ever known......I hope you will do your best to push the London production of Brown with Dean, and try to have a talk with Coward about it." He signs "Yours in a hurry, Gene."

O'Neill was referring to Noel Coward who had just had a successful show on Broadway and would be returning to London. With a flash of humour he wrote to his friend Macgowan about the money owed to him, "My advice is: stealing my royalties from the GV, abscond on the

Actor with mask in *Lazarus Laughed*. (*Yale University*)

first boat and come here! I will stake you to the fare as your collector's commission, and in spite of my professional ire will bed and feed you as if you were an honest man and not a manager."

Seven hundred miles out to sea on the Rock as Bermudians affectionately called their island, the ship arriving with the mail and newspapers never ceased to be exciting. A great surprise came for O'Neill at the end of March and he notes, "Letter from Yale offering me Litt D. degree." After thinking it over for several days he "wrote declining Yale degree if have to go through ceremony of bestowal." He did not send the letter after second thoughts. He hated public appearances but "then reconsidered—might be worth while going through." O'Neill had attended Princeton for one year and had taken a playwrighting course at Harvard, but that was the extent of his university experiences. He decided to accept. The presentation would be late in June, which fitted perfectly with summer plans.

One day O'Neill walked up the outside stone staircase to his cedar-beamed room, thinking with satisfaction of the telephone call he had just received from the Cable and Wireless Company telling him his royalties had been paid. He went in to write yet another letter to his friend Macgowan to tell him *Lazarus Laughed* was finished, ready to be typed and reviewed. "In the meantime, I am going to get started on the lady play *Strange Interlude* if I can—and my creative urge is all for going on .... As for Lazarus, what shall I say? It is so near to me yet that I feel as if it were pressed against my eyes and I couldn't see it. I wish you were around to take a look before I go over it. Certainly it contains the highest writing I have done.... Certainly it uses masks as they have never been used before and with an intensely dramatic meaning that really should establish them as sound and true medium in the modern theatre. Certainly, I know of no play like Lazarus at all, and I know of none who can play Lazarus at all—the lead I mean. Who can we get to laugh as one would laugh who had completely lost, even from the depths of the unconscious, all traces of the Fear of Death?"

The playwright had "many new and richer notions." One notion he had (nothing to do with the ones he wrote to his mentor) was to affect the O'Neill family to the present day. The hoped-for long lease on Bellevue was not possible. He and Agnes decided to look for a house to buy in Bermuda.

Spithead

Chapter 5

*The family buys Spithead, a big house on the water needing much repair.
The playwright works, enjoys swimming and suffers the birth pangs of*
Strange Interlude..

The restless and moody O'Neill who moved from one place to another liked the idea of seeking some permanence in Bermuda. He was sure it was a place where his creative abilities would flourish. He had written a complete play his first year on the island and would finish *Lazarus Laughed* before he left at the end of this second visit. The mild climate suited him and the sea was perfect. He liked some of the local people although he would poke fun and say there was no one with the intelligence above that of a land crab! Bermuda seemed to have many advantages for all the family and, very importantly for him; it was a place where he had managed to control his drinking for the first time.

Agnes ever adapting to O'Neill's whims and moods, liked Bermuda too, finding it an easy place to run a large household with pleasant servants and plenty of sunny weather. She could remember how poor they had been when she and O'Neill married in 1918.

They met in the excitement of creative life in Greenwich Village at the end of the Great War. She was a Bohemian young woman earning her meagre living by writing. She had left Barbara at home with her parents and gone to New York to find the bright lights. She had found an astonishing man, a genius, who drunk or sober she adored. She coped with the violence and temper when he was taken over by what he described as the "companiable intensely dramatic phantoms and obsessions which with caressing claws in my heart and brain, led me for weeks at a time down the ever changing vistas of the no-mans-land between the DTs and reality".

At Bellevue she did not often think of those days and the subsequent move to Provincetown where Shane was born in their tiny house on October 20th, 1919 and they gave him the Irish names Shane Rudraighe. It was at this time O'Neill received the heady offer from the Greenwich Village Theatre in New York to produce his plays. For the young couple it was bitter-sweet success as O'Neill had to go back there for rehearsals to immerse himself in the rushing stream of the theatre world. With the baby the money problems of a move back to New York could not be surmounted. They were very much in love and wrote to each other every day when separated. In the long winter months he was away, his letters ended with loving messages. He warmed her heart with, "I love you, My Own! A million for you to divide with Shane, I love you Gene."

As a couple they had been inseparable-physically and spiritually in love. Agnes quoted Blake's lines to him from *Love's Secret:*

> Never seek to tell thy love,
> Love that never told can be.

But O'Neill did seek to tell his love. He wrote every day, letters telling about the theatre, his struggles to get his plays produced, his loneliness, ending with passionate protestations of longing and love. Agnes replied with news of Shane and how much she missed him and pretended after she had gone to bed that he was still there. Mrs. Clark stayed in the house to help with the baby.

Agnes writes how handsome the nurse thought he looked the day he left and how concerned she was that O'Neill did not wear a wedding ring and therefore might be subject to advances from the opposite sex. The influenza epidemic had swooped down reaping the souls of millions in untimely deaths. O'Neill writes how ill he is and fears he has caught the 'flu'. Agnes begs him to take care of himself because she does not know how she could live without him.

In the dark hours of winter, she has foreboding thoughts. Her imagination flares. She has complete faith in him as a playwright, but fears when the inevitable success comes something dreadful will spoil the enjoyment of it for them. From a youthful heart admiration pours forth about how wonderful and fine he is. She dreams he has gone back to Catholicism; she worries about his drinking and begs him not to get into any fights. The first responsibilities of parenthood had closed in on

Agnes and O'Neill and they consoled each other with letters, his with theatre news and constant complaints of ill health and hers with news of the baby, fantasies and how domestic expenses could not be kept under $20 a week.

In the bright sunlight of Bermuda thoughts of those days did not intrude on Agnes' comfortable life. She did not find island life conducive to working at her writing and gave it up. However she had her family about her and had learned to live with a genius. Their love might not be as rapturous as it once was but he could only love one woman at a time and he loved her. He was much too busy to be a philanderer. He needed Agnes and when they were parted he still wrote warm and loving letters every day.

Suddenly in Bermuda the O'Neills heard of an eighteenth-century estate called Spithead on the shore in Warwick Parish that had come on the market. They decided to go and look at it.

THE SHIP EXPERIMENT HEZEKIAH FRITH MASTER

The *Experiment*, built of Bermuda cedar by Hezekiah Frith, privateer about 1790, shown anchored off Spithaed. *(Captain Musson)*

Captain Hezekiah Frith, a Privateer, had built the great stone house about 1780. It stood, at the head of a spit of land on the waters of Granaway Deep and was named for the famous Spithead in England.

A view of Hamilton was far to the east while to the north and west were uninhabited islands. Croswell Bowen in his book *The Curse of the Misbegotten* refers to Spithead as "a big stone palace".

O'Neill's imagination was captured by the estate, especially its position on the water, fulfilling his ideal of "water sports and outdoors". At one time the property stretched from one shore to the other a mile and a half away. In 1926 about 17 acres went with the house, its cottages and outbuildings. Much of the land was hillside wooded with cedars, while up over the hill lay fertile planting fields, in the charge of a farmer.

The whole place was run down and the main house was very dilapidated - so much so that the floors upstairs were going through. The architectural features that had remained for a century and a half were grand. The chimneys, the huge domed water tank, the separate kitchen building with its wide fireplace and bake ovens were among the countless treasures with which Agnes and O'Neill fell in love. The wharf was crumbling and the gardens were a blue tangle of morning glory. The place belonged to an American, a Mrs. Brown who lived in the United States and had not been to Bermuda for years. Nothing had been done for some twelve years since before the Great War. The old caretaker let people land at the crumbling wharf and let the coloured children from over the hill swim there in the summertime.

The O'Neills made an offer. They would have to get permission from the Governor in Council to own the property. Would-be purchasers of land in Bermuda had to furnish references from home, both financial and social. This was to prevent criminals and undesirable entrepreneurs from establishing themselves in the twenty-square-mile colony.

Nothing interfered with O'Neill's daily concentration or his work at Bellevue. He was enthused about *Lazarus*, sure it was the best writing he had done. Arthur and Barbara Gelb, in their biography, *O'Neill*, express lively opinions on the play they called "unactable". They felt the big, laughing Lazarus, so sure he had overcome death, had turned out to be an unconvincing hero because O'Neill himself did not believe death could be overcome. The Gelbs grant that some passages in the play are finely poetic and speculate that O'Neill who loved the play so much was possibly carried away by his own imaginative writing. O'Neill spent weeks reviewing or what he refers to as "going over" and was finally able to record "finished going over last scene—will call that play done now—think it fine stuff but know no one will ever produce it".

It was the season of Easter with its message of eternal life, when O'Neill was reviewing *Lazarus*. Bermudians remember their dead at that time and go to the churchyards and decorate the graves of their loved ones or ancestors they never knew. The graves are dug out of the coral rock and covered over with slabs of whitewashed coral which dazzle in the sunshine against the green lawns. People of all ages bring big bunches of flowers and arrange them in containers on the graves. Even small children join in putting flowers and babies watch from their prams. Old people tendering their bouquets hide any trembling feelings knowing in the back of their minds that physical death has not been overcome and some day, not too distant, they will inevitably be entombed themselves. The spring sunshine gleams on the scarlet amaryllis, the waxen white Easter lilies, the sweet peas, the spears of snapdragons and a myriad of other flowers in many colours brought from home gardens. All classes of society exchange polite greetings and their duty done, leave the vigil of Easter to the bedecked scene which will be softened by the evening starlight and dew.

A field of Easter lilies. Many buds were exported to the United States and a bunch went every spring to the Royal Family in England. *(Bermuda Archives)*

In the anguished drunken year of 1925 O'Neill had conceived a play called *Strange Interlude,* which would run to nine acts. Ever pressing on, in the last weeks of spring of 1926 he started on his great work. He says, "(looks damned interesting - good stuff...)".

Local people were not backward in telling the O'Neills about the ghosts at Spithead. The most important of the phantoms was Hezekiah himself, a privateer, a legal pirate in his day. The king, George III, had given Letters of Marque to certain sailing-ship captains to attack the ships of France, with whom England was at war. Thus, private vessels helped the Royal Navy police the seas in exchange for booty. In the course of his normal trading along the East Coast of the United States and down in the West Indies, Hezekiah took a French prize. On board was a young French woman whom he brought back to Bermuda. She died at Spithead, and Agnes has been quoted as saying she saw the veiled and shadowy figure in the long gallery upstairs. Also drifting about of a night the O'Neills were told, was Hezekiah's son, who had the misfortune to be killed by a bolt of lightning while out in a small boat on Granaway Deep. In life he was a disappointed man overshadowed by the powerful character of his father, and in death an apparition not often seen.

Perhaps stories of these ghosts appealed to O'Neill's imagination. In *Strange Interlude,* Nina describes a visit to her husband's old gloomy home in upstate New York, "It isn't haunted by anything at all-and ghosts of some sort are the only life a house has, like our minds, you know. They (the ghosts) drifted away over the grass, whisps of mist between the apple trees". In *The Emperor Jones,* in a chilling episode when the hero is alone in the dark forest, he is tormented by the ghosts of the guard he killed when part of a chain gang: "I kills you, you white debil, if it's de last thing I evah does. Ghost or debil, I kill you agin". The stage directions say, "He frees his revolver and fires point blank at the ghostly guard's back. Instantly the walls of the forest close in from both sides, the road and the phantom figures of the convict gang are blotted out in an enshrouding darkness".

To carry out their enthusiastic plans for the restoration of Spithead the O'Neills engaged the American architect Frederick Hill. He had designed the Prince George Hotel in New York and was currently overseeing the completion of a large house in Bermuda for the Blair family from Tuxedo Park. The O'Neills would leave all arrangements for carrying out their ideas to Hill, since they were going to spend the

O'Neill designed the welcoming steps going up to the front door at Spithead. (*Bermudian Magazine*)

summer in Maine.

The O'Neills were partial to the unique architecture of Bermuda and wanted the old cedar work and eighteenth–century features preserved. Agnes wanted a kitchen wing added, so the old kitchen cottage could be adapted for staff. O'Neill wanted a tennis court. After realizing how much work keeping the grass court at Bellevue involved, he decided on a concrete court-quite the fashion at the time. He also wanted the wharf repaired and the bulkhead reinforced to shelter his two boats. He wanted a welcoming arms stone staircase constructed to lead up to the second floor, where the large rooms of the house were and where the front door would be. The downstairs had lower ceilings as, in Hezekiah's day, it was used to stow gear from his two frigates and contraband from his privateering raids. His family lived upstairs. O'Neill wanted the smaller house, quaintly called the "dance hall" on the deeds, fixed up right away. All this they wanted done for $7,000.

From the start, prices were not hard and fast and would later become hectically muddled. Hill pointed out that any overall estimate to renovate an old house was impossible to get. A precise and meticulous man, he wanted to make his fees clear and wrote: "As to my commission... my fee is 6% on the total cost of the work, this covers drawings, memo certificates, obtaining estimates, making out contracts and issuing certificates when payments are due the contractor".

The Hills owned a fine equipage and Mrs. Hill with her daughter were often seen spanking along in their carriage. They lived at Pembroke Hall, a large house which they rented from the Dill family, situated on the water at the Foot of the Lane where it turns to go into Hamilton. To reach Spithead, Hill would have to drive in his carriage or get on his "wheel" and bicycle the three and a half miles. Hill wrote, "I do not regularly superintend the work but make such visits of supervision as I think necessary and my charge for this is £2-0-0 per visit".

Houses in Bermuda were roofed with coral slate, which on large estates in the old days was quarried on the property. The large building blocks of coral rock were likewise sawn from a hillside. Two men sat facing each other with the coral stone in between them. They had a long saw with a handle at either end. It was skilled work to draw the saw back and forth, fashioning the blocks of coral slate to the exact measurements. The heavy slate at Spithead is laid on cedar rafters, secured with eighteenth-century mortar mixed with turtle oil. As is the custom on all

Bermuda houses, the roof is guttered to conduct the rain to the down pipes, which are connected to the stone tank. Rainwater was the only water in Bermuda except for brackish wells. Therefore, the huge stone roof, so neatly made with overlapping coral slate and white-washed for purity, was designed to catch the precious rain water. In time of drought there could be a serious shortage of water. The dance bands and ukulele players had a new tune out at the time, which was very apropos; it went, "It ain't gonna rain no mo' no mo' so how in heck can I wash my neck if it ain't gonna rain no mo'?"

Down pipes sloped from the gutters conducting the water into the great domed tank where it was stored. A door allowed inspection of the water level as eyes became adjusted to the gloomy interior of the watery cathedral. To keep the water pure, no light was allowed to shine in because algae would not grow in the dark. Hezekiah had built the tank large in order to have plenty of water for his ships. He records it held a measure of 500 hogsheads (about 7,000 gallons). Before sailing, the huge barrels on board had to be filled. The water level was low when the O'Neills bought the house for the down pipes from the roof were rotten and holed so that the water spilled, wasted on the ground. New pipes were the first priority.

The water had to be brought into the house. In the old days it was hauled in buckets from the tank and taken into the house, where it stood ready to be dipped for its many uses. Hill was installing one of the new electric pumps that would force the water up into the galvanised iron tanks placed high up from whence it would flow by gravity to the taps. Laundry was still done in the backyard in the big iron tubs and rubbed up and down on the corrugated glass washboards. It dried in the sun, hung out in the sweet-scented air off the sea.

A relic from another era, the old privy still stood on the dock, built of stone with a tall-pointed roof with a ball on top. Over the edge of the wharf behind the privy, a channel had been dug in the rocks below to enable the tides to wash away the waste. A member of the Frith family tells how his ancestors, when they received a call of nature, would seize their fishing lines, hurry to settle on the wooden seats and fish out of the window. There must have been other privies on the estate but only the one two-holer remained. A one-holer had one seat, a two-holer two seats and so on even up to four seats. As to fishing out of the windows, it is hard to imagine such composure for underneath the seats on the spattered walls lived many large cockroaches that crawled up sometimes to investigate the "moon" occupying the seat. In those long ago days before insecticides blazing sheets of newspaper were dropped down to kill cockroaches.

Hezekiah had two partners, also sea captains, with whom he had an agreement to share equally in all booty taken after the King's share had been deducted. He had a large storehouse built on the wharf. The story goes that under the floor a secret tunnel was dug that had a hidden trapdoor. The subterranean passage came up by a fireplace inside the house, enabling small things to be secretly brought in from the warehouse. By O'Neill's day the warehouse had disappeared and the tunnel was never found.

Sequestered in his cottage at Bellevue with a glimpse of the ocean from the window and the distant roar of the surf in his ears, the birth pangs of *Strange Interlude* taxed the playwright. The play seems anything but an interlude in the ordinary sense of the word, spanning as it does the adult lives of the protagonists. The play, in nine acts, is written in two parts and is sometimes produced as a two-day performance or divided by a long dinner interval. O'Neill was trying a new idea, the "speech-thought method," where the actors converse but in lengthy asides say what they really think. The personalities of these thespians are thus doubly revealed.

O'Neill had thought of spending the summer back in Provincetown where he owned an old abandoned coast guard station at Peaked Hill. He feared, however, it might make him sad to go back. He loved it but he wanted to shake off all past connotations. "The old truth is no longer the truth," he wrote, "too many 'somethins' hide in the corners". Bermuda had been the beginning of change and now he wanted a new summer place. "What I need for my new voyage is fresh winds and new ports of call. . . .an opportunity for interesting associations with new people, combined with water sports and out doors." It was almost as if he had a premonition of the changes Maine would bring in his life.

When the middle of June arrived at Bellevue, the poincianas blossomed to make their scarlet canopies. The cicadas were singing in the trees, the bluebird fledglings were finding their own grubs on the lawns and the air was sweet with the perfume of oleanders. Bermudians were boating. The yachts taking part in the Newport to Bermuda Race had crossed the Gulf Stream and were about to arrive. The O'Neills were off to the United States. They would stay a few days in New York and visit the Macgowans in Brewster, Massachusetts. O'Neill was going to receive his honorary degree at Yale University. By the end of June the family would be installed in Loon Lodge, at the water's edge, among the pines of Belgrade Lakes in Maine.

Before leaving Bellevue, Agnes and Gaga toiled to pack all the belongings, some to be left behind since when they returned to Bermuda, Spithead would be ready, and the O'Neills would move into their own home. O'Neill travelled with piles of manuscripts and books that he packed himself. The maids would stay on to clean the house after they left. A horse-drawn wagon came the day before sailing for the large pieces of luggage. As they stepped the next day from the imposing carriage at Number One shed on Front Street, spectators admired the family. The O'Neills mounted the gangplank to the S.S. *Fort St. George*, the famous author with his striking wife secure and smiling carrying her infant girl, his son and Barbara shepherded along by the indispensable Gaga.

If the seas were calm the ocean voyage in the small ship was a pleasant interlude. Many of the sixty some passengers knew each other or met taking meals at various officers' tables. On deck the stewards served "beef tea" at eleven in the morning. Passengers amused themselves playing shuffleboard or deck quoits. A young Bermudian lady of prominent family, Miss Dora Gilbert, was honoured, as were the O'Neills, with an invitation to sit at the Captain's table. Children and nurses in those days took their meals at an earlier sitting.

In the afternoon, Miss Gilbert, reclining in her deck chair, remembers she was surprised to see O'Neill in charge of Oona, who was taking her infant steps along the promenade deck, not helped by the gentle rolling of the ship, lifting and falling to the waves. He came over to Dora and asked if she would mind looking after Oona for a bit. He assured her the baby would be no trouble as he would tie her to the deck chair, which he promptly did and made off. "He was tall and dark, with intense dark eyes", she says, and added, "he sometimes smiled".

Chapter 6

The family summers at Belgrade Lakes, Maine, returning to Bermuda
in the autumn.
The playwright labours over *Strange Interlude* beside the lake.
Carlotta Monterey, a beautiful actress appears.

At Loon Lodge the sunshine filtered down through the pines beside the
tranquil lake, and it was not hard to imagine in the shadowed woods the
misty figure of Hiawatha, fringed and feathered, melting away, his
moccasined feet seeking an old Indian trail. There was plenty to fire the
imagination of a small boy and Shane's happiness was complete when
he found the lake teeming with fish. Oona flourished in the refreshing
air and cool nights. Her diapers blew on the laundry line in the scented
breeze. The eleven year old Barbara was glad to see the handsome
Eugene, Jr. arrive and promptly fell in love with him. O'Neill wrote to
Macgowan "we're a fat family".

O'Neill welcomed Eugene, Jr. With this child of his youth he felt
more of a rapport than he would ever feel with the others. The boy was
just finishing high school and his father was gratified that his son would
be going to Yale. When he had received his honorary degree from Yale,
O'Neill had been deeply affected to be hailed at the great university as
"a creative contributor of the new and moving forms to one of the oldest

of the arts and as the first American playwright to receive both wide and serious recognition upon the stage of Europe". It warmed Eugene, Jr.'s heart to be part of the family where the plentiful meals were a reunion and where an enjoyable confusion reigned.

A bolt from the blue arrived in this domestic scene. O'Neill only entered personal events of prime importance in his working diary and on July 15, 1926, he wrote "Met Carlotta (Monterey) - 1st time since a moment's introduction at the *Hairy Ape* rehearsals!"

The playwright and the actress on the lake in Maine. *(Louis Shaeffer)*

The beautiful actress whom he had not seen for four years was staying nearby and was part of the summer social scene. Photographs taken at the time show a classic beauty. Her fine features suggest a romantic nature of subtle sensuality mixed with mystery. She gives the impression she is a prize worth winning. At the O'Neill home beside the lake in Maine she posed, actress-like, for a photograph, leaning against a tree trunk her figure well displayed in a tight top and short shorts, a daring outfit for the era. In another picture she stands, hands on hips, in the bow of a rowing boat, with O'Neill sitting amidships on the thwart, ready to take her for a pull around the lake.

In more formal photographs, she is shown wearing clothes obviously expensive, of simple elegance. She was about the same age as O'Neill, in her mid-thirties, and a lady with a past. She had been married three times and had a daughter who lived with Carlotta's mother. O'Neill's diary relates that Carlotta returned to Belgrade Lakes in August and again in September. In one entry he puts "saw Carlotta again (slavey b.s.)" Did he mean she had captured him body and soul?

At Loon Lodge, O'Neill's work went on uninterrupted in spite of Carlotta. He laboured at *Strange Interlude* unceasingly, experiencing great difficulties with it throughout July, but in early August he writes, "seems coming now".

The architect Hill from Bermuda visited them in late July while on a trip to the United States and enjoyed the "cool and quiet of Maine", and the hospitality of the O'Neills. Upon his return he wrote letters, constantly, regarding the improvements to Spithead. Permission to buy the property had been granted by the Governor, but the current owner, a Mrs. Brown who lived in the United States was dilatory is signing the deeds. Consequently, Hill was legally unable to send workmen on the land. Such were the delays that he was not able to start until October. O'Neill is reputed to have paid $17,000 for the property. In present times 60 years later the value, were the estate still intact, would be three to four million dollars. To top off Hill's renovation problems, there was a hurricane. He wrote, "The hurricane was a bad one, caused more damage than they have ever had; driving from Hamilton to Tucker's Town I counted 70 houses more or less injured so was glad Spithead came through so well—another section of the sea wall came down due to its being built of stone instead of concrete." The eye of the hurricane had passed over with winds up to 114 mph.

O'Neill left the correspondence with Hill to Agnes that summer. She wrote long letters often asking him to make changes and to cable back what he thought. Money was of prime concern and she urged him to modify plans in order to cut expenses. The huge stone roof was blamed for a large part of the cost. Supported by cedar rafters made from trimmed whole tree trunks, the stone slates were held on by cedar stringers attached to the rafters with iron nails. In a century and a half, the nails had rusted away and the heavy stone slates were in danger of sliding off. Old turtle oil mortar was all that held them together. Repairs had to be done.

Hill was one up in the wrangles over expenses when he wrote, "The main house roof held as the storm hit the end that had been fixed and not the part that was weak". Agnes, writing one of her confused letters, wanted a door where a window was and a window where a door was. Hill assured her it would be less expensive and more practical to leave the plan as it was. But on the whole it became obvious only a small portion of the alterations and repairs could be carried out before the O'Neills returned. Work was stopped on the main house to get the "Dance Hall" finished in time. Even this proved impossible, and the O'Neills would have to rent another place for a few months. Hill persevered with detail: "I will never use an enamelled drain board unless compelled to do so—they are subject to chipping and cause more broken dishes than they are worth." Hill ordered a wooden drain board.

Confusion ensued until Hill in exasperation wrote to Agnes in his neat handwriting, "I regret very much that my services have caused so much dissatisfaction… and if you desire, I will retire in favour of any one else whom you may elect." In the meantime, he would carry on and he would like them to settle his cable bill.

In Maine, the leaves had turned their glorious colours and had fallen by mid-October when the O'Neills left the chilly lake. Back in New York, O'Neill's mind was far from drain boards and the muddle at Spithead. His early prizewinning play *Beyond the Horizon* was being revived by the Actors' Theatre and would open at the Mansfield after he had reached Bermuda. Carlotta was in town. Agnes, once again parted from O'Neill, was in Ridgefield with the children. It was too expensive to have everyone in New York. O'Neill went out to Ridgefield for a few days and it was settled that Agnes would precede him with the children and Gaga to Bermuda, where a house called Belmere, that was within walking distance of Spithead, had been leased. She could supervise the restoration of the property and he would be down towards the end of November.

Back in the city O'Neill attended rehearsals. He took Carlotta to lunch, to dinner, to the symphony and she accompanied him to the rehearsals. Carlotta's "immaculate and tastefully furnished" apartment was at 20 East Sixty-seventh Street, and it was there O'Neill went for "tea and sympathy". It was known that Carlotta had money and this impressed O'Neill, who was always trying to improve his standard of living and often found himself in financial difficulties. Agnes, although a disorganized and untidy housekeeper, did keep account of household expenses and often went without herself so life could run more smoothly for O'Neill.

After the long summer with children, family and guests at Loon Lodge, it was a change for O'Neill to be the man about town. The undivided attention of an elegant, adoring lady with plenty of leisure was irresistible. Carlotta bought O'Neill clothes at Abercrombie & Fitch and went with him to Macy's to buy a kayak that he wanted sent down to Spithead. The evening before he sailed, a cozy dinner at Carlotta's went on until two thirty in the morning by his own confession to his diary.

On board the S.S. *Fort St. George* as she pulled away from the pier, O'Neill was at odds with himself, down in his cabin and painfully resisting drinking. Warm memories of the early morning parting with Carlotta were with him as he sat down to write her a letter: "Dearest She's starting to roll now, off the Hook [Sandy Hook is where the great swell of the Atlantic is first felt outside New York Harbour]. I remember in my sailor days what a thrill of living it gave me. It meant a release then, an end of an old episode and the birth of a new." With heavy humour he laments the loss of his youth in imaginary conversations with characters from an early "sea play".

"Quite like the Hairy Ape, that long-drowned self of mine, who comes back to haunt my loneliest bitterest hours." Dramatically he continues, "a hell of a lonely longing for you. And a desperation too blindly suffering for the saving vision of any hope. God has turned his back and slammed the door and all the prison is in darkness" And then, "only just now you seem so far away, so lost to me. If I could only kiss you again, Carlotta—"

The following evening he writes again for Carlotta had sent him a Marconigram to the ship. "It was darling of you to send it. It was as if your presence became suddenly apparent in my cabin and I could hear your voice saying that 'everything will come out as we wish it," He had sent her roses, "I hope the roses pleased you." He thought of her letters arriving in Bermuda. "I think I shall have to tell the truth right from the start down here. It will be kinder to all in the end…. Oh, I don't know what I'll do. I'm so tortured now I can't trust my own judgment. In a final burst of emotion he cries, "beloved one, whose heart is now my own heart, whose wish is my wish, whose will and way are my will and way! My love, I adore you ! Do not forget me! Gene

He sent a wire, "IT IS LONELY MY LOVE GENE"

Sleep was elusive on the voyage. As the ship neared Bermuda, the restless playwright could go up at first light to join other passengers on deck to watch the pilot gig approach and the remarkable feat of the pilot coming on board. It was not uncommon for these pilot-crews, ten rowers in all, to go fifty or sixty miles off Bermuda, looking for custom. There were several gigs and pilots all in competition with each other. The first one viewed by a ship got the contract to bring the steamer in through the reefs and hence made the pilotage fee. With the *St. George* hove-to a rope ladder was lowered from near the bow and the crew in the rising and falling gig waited to seize hold if it. The pilot slowly climbed the ladder as it swung outward from the ship's side. When the vessel rolled the other way the ladder, with the clinging man, swung inward slamming against the ship's hull. With the pilot safely aboard, the passengers waved good-bye to the rowers left behind on the heaving sea, the oars rising and dipping. The distant helmsman steered by instinct to find the island out of sight below the horizon. Leaning on the rail, watching the gig in the trough of the waves, O'Neill could moodily remember very different voyages of long ago when he slept in a bunk in the forecastle with the rest of the crew.

After all the flutter of his romance in New York, O'Neill was glad to be once again in the bosom of his family. He wrote "Well here we are — stopping temporarily in a cottage near our place." The workmen had not finished the smaller house nor had the furniture arrived. "Our Spithead will be a wonder of a spot once it's done. It's ideal for me. I've been swimming every day…"

He confided to Macgowan, "Yet I'm not what you call perfectly at peace with God. The two days' voyage was a beautiful little minor hell. The cost of living seems exorbitant. One was tempted to refuse to pay the bill. I envy simple souls to whom life is always this or that. If the this *and* that, the this-that desire-more than desire, need! that slow-poisons the soul with complicated contradictions… And it is good to be home again. And lucky I left when I did—for I love her and them and my home and nothing could ever take their place but—Oh Christ there are always other things—on the other side of the hills—the curse of being an extremist is that every ideal remains single and alone, demanding all - or - nothing or destruction. Oh balls! 'What haunted, haunting ghosts we are.'"

At Belmere O'Neill was soon at work on *Marco Millions*, which was to be published. When the book came out O'Neill inscribed a copy for Agnes with the words of Kublai the Great Kaan [*This was O'Neill's spelling.*] praising his granddaughter Princess Kukachin: "you have been a golden bird singing beside the black river - the river of a man's life." He returned to *Lazarus Laughed*, which he recorded "is immensely improved." He always loved this fanciful work and even hoped it might be produced in Russian. He urged Macgowan to get in touch with Chaliapin in person. If the celebrated actor and singer played the role of Lazarus in Russian and the rest of the cast spoke English, the audience would understand the laughing risen man just as well, O'Neill commented with rare humour.

The November days were cool, but hot in the mid-day sun. The kayak arrived and he sent a picture of himself sitting in it to Carlotta, "This is my kayak canoe-Eskimo model in which I have a lot of fun paddling about. It is a fine rough weather boat, small as it is, and one can go almost anywhere in it." When the dramatist needed a rest from writing he skimmed off in his little boat to the uninhabited islands off Spithead. In their centre lies a lagoon called Paradise Bay, where kingfishers spend the winter. On one island among the cedars lay the graves of the Boer prisoners, who had died far from their homeland in South Africa. The soldiers had been brought to Bermuda during the Boer War at the turn of the century and imprisoned on the islands. A disused Royal Naval isolation hospital for fever patients stood overlooking the lagoon. Some of the small islands are named after the letters of the Greek alphabet, which O'Neill had been memorising the previous winter at Bellevue.

He also often paddled along the Warwick shore down to the Inverurie Hotel. Sometimes, as he passed Hinson's Island, he could see Hal Kitchener, who had served in the Royal Flying Corps, and was Lord Kitchener's nephew, readying his small seaplane for a pleasure flight over Bermuda. O'Neill was happy with his little boat but when he watched the yacht races in the Great Sound, "Daddy" still needed a yacht for himself.

Letters came from Carlotta. She had not yet received his impassioned letters written on the ship and wrote in a calm fashion, taking

O'Neill on the rocks at Spithead had written on his bathing suit:
"To Carlotta with my love Gene". (*Yale University*)

some of the love-wind out of his sails. He replied, "Dear Carlotta: It was grand to get your two letters by the last boat. The steamer service to this isle is for some reason temporarily disrupted and there is only one mail a week—so one looks forward to it with double expectations... I have read your letters many times. Evidently they were written before you had received either of mine. They were very good medicine for me. They bought me back to earth. They imparted to me some of your own calm—which I badly needed to get back to 'living as usual' and settling to work again. You see I had a training the exact opposite to yours. It was extremely undisciplined.... I have always been either hilariously shooting in on the crest of the wave or else bogged down up to my neck in a swamp. The dry, warm, sure-footed middle ground was the one place where I never was taught to walk. So I finally escaped on to the one place of my work where I can always dance and drown and be reborn to dance and drown again. When work wouldn't come I had to escape via masks of solitude, alcoholic and otherwise, provided only they were excessive.... I'm feeling wonderfully again—physically speaking. The swimming and the lying in the sun can do wonders for me in even a few days... This letter sounds stilted and self-conscious. I was never meant to be 'wise and adult,' I guess. I'd rather, if I could, be very young and unwise—or very dead.... Good night Carlotta—and my love. Gene."

The following week he wrote again answering another letter from Carlotta in which she asked him what he meant when he wrote he has been perfectly frank. ("Aglow with naive honesty" he had told Agnes about Carlotta.) He replied: "just that! As soon as I reached here I told Agnes exactly how I had felt about leaving you. I said I loved you. I also said, with equal truth that I loved her. Does this sound idiotic to you? I hope not!.... But I suppose you are curious about Agnes. She has been very fine about it. She has offered to do anything I want—set me free, etc., etc. However, it is ridiculous to imagine one can set oneself free by one's own efforts.... Good night Dear! sometimes I smell your hair again, to feel your lips —. Those are wonderful times - but torturing. I hope you get my flowers on Christmas. They are a symbol of what might have been—or may be. Roses are as wonderful—or as banal—as love. It all depends what we make of them. Gene."

Carlotta had been writing diligently, for three letters arrived after Christmas. In this case it did seem as though distance together with torrid love letters were making the hearts grow fonder. O'Neill wrote,

"I feel like a dog for not having gotten off a letter to you sooner.... Three of your letters arrived since my last to you. I have read and reread them —and gotten myself into a terrible state of guilty conscience and self-loathing. It seems at times as if all the suffering I find in your letters were my fault - that I ought to tell you to forget about me, to go on with your life as if I never came into it. And yet I can't do that! Can't!"

Carlotta Monterey was born in California in 1888, of part Danish descent, and christened Hazel Neilson Tharsing. Such a name scarcely suited her dark romantic beauty, so by the time her love for O'Neill began to bud she had long since adopted her stage name. During her third marriage, she formed a relationship with and eventually became the mistress of, James Speyer, "an elderly Wall Street banker... he made Carlotta one of his private philanthropies by establishing a trust fund which provided her, to the end of her life, with an annual income that averaged close to fourteen thousand dollars." It is said that Carlotta told O'Neill she had inherited the money from an aunt.

He referred to her past when he wrote, "yes. I know you have been much—'what men call loved.' And I am jealous of those 'strange hours and months.' It is a pity every love cannot be that first love which is alone without regret. Afterwards, there is always the past—the past of each which lives a sinister new life in the other's mind! Even when you know there was never a love of 'gentleness and sweetness and exulta-tion and spiritual fire.' Carlotta had written a letter to Agnes. O'Neill reports, "Agnes thought your note to her fine. And I—I can't tell you how fine I think your attitude is about all this. You make me feel like some particularly hopeless species of worm." He tells Carlotta how he has been swimming, rowing, and feeling fine. He refers to Spithead "our house will be a peach when it is finished off – (if the money lasts that long!) Shane is eagerly awaiting your gift. The books haven't arrived yet—nor the candy—it seems everything was sent to a sub-post office. Christmas demoralizes the service down here.... Good'bye, Dear! Forgive me for loving you, for your love for me. It seems to have brought you nothing but pain. But I couldn't help it ! You shouldn't be - so you! (write) Gene."

The family moved into the "Dance Hall," really a cottage, just before Christmas. Agnes was busy arranging her household. John Davis, a skillful carpenter who was in charge of the woodworking at Spithead, had a daughter called Hilda whom Agnes hired to help Gaga with the children. She engaged Lillian Trott to be the cook and her sister Dorothy as housemaid, two amiable young coloured women of reliable family. Agnes wanted to untangle the gardens, especially the walled winter garden behind the main house, where old-fashioned roses grew. She hired as gardener an aged coloured chap called Walter Scott, of whom she said "he would make a great character for a book." With five in staff Agnes was running what might be called an establishment.

Shane had his seventh birthday and the question of his schooling was a pressing matter. He spoke French with Gaga but she was not capable of teaching him his three R's. The O'Neills met Commander Ridgway and his wife Helena who had two daughters about the age of Shane and Oona. The English Commander, retired from the Royal Navy, stood tall and straight. Helena was a humorous diminutive lady of the Bermuda Gosling family. They were fans of A.A. Milne and nicknamed their girls Tigger and Piglet after Winnie the Pooh's friends. They had a governess and suggested that Shane join Tigger for lessons and that Oona should come to play with Piglet.

"Shane had a runny nose all the time," said Tigger now married to a prominent Charleston, North Carolina, lawyer. She reflected on the difficulty of mopping up the boy's nose in those pre-Kleenex days. "Oona was a dark wraith of a child," she said. The O'Neill children were amazed by Piglet's dog, Bustie, who sat in front of the Victrola and "sang". He pointed his nose upward and produced a wide rang of yowling, howling notes in time to the music. On a visit to the Ridgways, a young Hollywood actor and entrepreneur was enchanted by Bustie's "singing" and wanted to take him to the movie capital, where he was sure the dog would be a big success. The Ridgways decided the children's dog would be greatly missed and had better stay at home.

From O'Neill's point of view, as he wrote to Macgowan, it was such "a hell of an overcrowded time of it in the little house, that I am working in a bedroom with children, carpenters, plumbers, masons and whatever you have doing all sorts of telling chorus work in the near vicinity and it doesn't bother me much, which proves that I can't really be as artistic as the prints would have it. Also we are discovering that the average Bermuda artisan more than makes up for his lower wages by the longer he takes. It is a scream to watch them doing stills of men at labour - but the scream is of laughter only when they are working on the place next door. But the place will be a wonder when it is finally fixed up - absolutely ideal for me and will surely pay me big dividends in the work I shall do here. I love it." In a postscript he refers indirectly to his love affair, "There is lots I don't write. Emotionally I'm still up in the air. Perhaps this will be good for *Interlude* (author's thought!) but otherwise it hain't purty."

With the approach of Christmas he worried lest Macgowan had not received the check for "25 to get roses for Carlotta for X'mas... I am intending to start work in Strange Interlude" tomorrow - the 31 - one year on the wagon, my boy! I am going to drink fifty lime squashes watching the new year in and, at least, put my lunch in memory of the good old days." He had recently written regarding *Strange Interlude,* "with all that's inside me now I ought to be able to explode in that play in a regular blood letting by the time I get to it."

There is a beautiful small room upstairs in Spithead overlooking the water on three sides. The foreman, Johnson, a handsome light-skinned man, suggested he fix up this room in the main house where O'Neill could work in peace.

"Mrs O'Neill told us 'Mr, O'Neill is *never* to be disturbed'." recalls Hilda who then was the new nursemaid. "We were not allowed to go in to clean. We were not even to call him for lunch. When Mr. O'Neill wanted his lunch he would hang a white towel out of the window and we girls, who were looking out for it, took the food over."

O'Neill walked across after breakfast to the main house. The December days were cool and fickle. The gentle summer winds from the south had shifted to the northwest, bringing slashing squalls over Granaway Deep, sending the spray flying as the waves broke against the sea wall. As suddenly as they came, the winds subsided, the sun came out, and the water returned to a shimmer of turquoise blue, and on land the vegetation sparkled with raindrops.

Furniture for the two houses was sent down from Ridgefield, but Agnes had become interested in English antiques. Her taste was changing and O'Neill became interested too. Much fine furniture was brought home by Bermudians returning from England in the ships that plied directly to the Island sailing from Plymouth or Liverpool. Agnes started to collect. She studied early photographs of Bermudian houses and spotted a large cedar mantelpiece and was certain the one painted over in Spithead was the same. She was furious to find Hill had had it torn out and put it on the wood pile. Hill had little feeling for local things and O'Neill told him off. "It took two men a day to search thru the large piles of old lumber before they finally located the two other parts of the mantel. It took a cabinet maker several days to put it together again, finally revealing a very beautiful old cedar mantel."

To overcome the problem of fresh milk for the household and to save money, Agnes bought a cow for about fifteen pounds. Old Scott milked it night and morning and when the cow was flush, after calving, Lillian could set the extra milk, skim the cream and make cottage cheese from the curds. Agnes claimed O'Neill worked best when a bit annoyed so, Hilda says, she tethered the cow under his window and took the calf elsewhere. Cows are very maternal and bawl continuously when separated from their calves. Perhaps an erudite literary historian could tell how much such a disturbance affected *Strange Interlude*!

Worrying news came that Agnes' father, Edward R. Boulton, who was suffering from tuberculosis, had entered a sanitarium. O'Neill wrote a very kind letter, saying: "I have always, as I hope you know, had a very soft spot in my heart for you and a deep affection." He urged him to keep up his courage, and assured him that his old "pep" would soon be back. O'Neill had had tuberculosis himself as a very young man and had made a complete recovery.

Now at Spithead O'Neill never went on a bender and Agnes worried and wanted to compensate him for his deprivation. Life for O'Neill had indeed changed, so that he wanted to "rechristen Spithead, Water Wagon Manor. It is connected in my mind with sane living."

His neighbours next door at Fleetwood Manor were certainly not on the water wagon. Joel and Mary Huber, Main Line Philadelphians who loved to entertain, were amusing and exuberant. They often had the coloured musician Sydney Bean and his Twilight Quartet to sing and play their ukuleles for the distinguished Bermudians and visitors who thronged their parties. Agnes loved the family and was glad to have their daughter Peggy Anne as a companion for Shane. There were also two sons, Tommy and Joey, one older and one younger than their sister. O'Neill did not respond much to the light-hearted gaiety at their home. He was not good at small talk and found little to interest him in the people he met over the wall, although he liked Huber himself.

The wall marked the boundary between the two properties so that when Huber was in his garden he could hear what was going on at Spithead. He liked to regale his friends with stories about his famous neighbour.

"Now and then," he recounted, "O'Neill would start cursing something or someone. He could swear for twenty minutes and never repeat himself. Listening to him was a real education!" O'Neill impressed young William Davis with his language when he came to Spithead to help his carpenter father and in the evenings to walk his sister Hilda home. He says, "Swear! Mr.O'Neill had a very loud mouth when he was mad. He was a real 'man-o'-war' sailor. The tars from those warships could swear something terrible," he added.

It tickled Huber to recount, "O'Neill would walk with his hands behind his back and if you addressed him, he would only grunt.,"

"I was very young then but I do remember Mr. O'Neill, especially his broody eyes," says Peggy Anne, now Mrs. Robert J. Miller. "Mr O'Neill was always kind to children but he never was one to engage them in small talk. He would say good morning to us," she continued. "He used to come for a drink with my Dad when he had finished a play." She added, "I think it was for comic relief!"

Huber was a character, and sometimes he would over-indulge in his favourite *Canadian Club*. One day, as a result, he became very ill and his wife, alarmed, sent for the ambulance, which took him at a fast trot along Harbour Road. When it neared the entrance to the hospital, Huber had revived and he signalled the driver to stop. He got out, hailed a passing carriage and returned home to Fleetwood Manor.

On the whole, good nature prevailed on both sides of the boundary wall. The O'Neills were well liked by the people who worked on the place even allowing their children to come and swim or fish. They were optimistic and enthusiastic about Spithead.

O'Neill had written Carlotta that he was divided in two, one half belonged to her and the other half to Agnes and the children whom he also loved. For him Spithead represented his home and ideal work place. For Agnes, Spithead was not only the hope of a secure family life but was far from New York isolating her husband from his *amour* while she was in a stronger position of an in place wife and mother. There was a common bond, a feeling of stability and satisfaction as the restoration proceeded. The dilapidated old porch across the front of the house was gone and the welcoming arms steps to the front door were going up. O'Neill had designed the steps himself adapting them from those he had seen on old Bermuda houses. They welcome guests to this day. The tennis court was progressing although he took Wm. Bluck & Co. to task when the paint on the concrete bleached out. (William Bluck was the Mayor of Hamilton and The Speaker of the House of Assembly.) Burland's who had bought the paint and put it on protested, when O'Neill refused to pay for it, saying only one coat could be done as Mrs

O'Neill was in a hurry as she was having a tennis party the next day! Two coats were necessary and the paint had proved all right on courts in Hamilton.

O'Neill looked forward to having the cottage to himself with his manuscripts and books. When they finally moved into the big house they found much careless and unfeeling work had been done. Hill was proving to be a most unsatisfactory choice of architect. He felt no exhilaration for the job and was unable to inspire those who worked with him to feel the importance of the restoration of this treasure of old Bermudian architecture. To O'Neill and Agnes it was truly important. On the other hand every step of the way both O'Neill and Agnes protested the expense, Burland the contractor was constantly chivvied and Hill run ragged trying to get fixed prices. O'Neill's anger, though, was justified by much dreadful work and he wrote a tremendous letter with 18 numbered complaints to Burland. (All walls whether stone or lath had to be plastered to a smooth finish.) No. 15. reads, "Plastering in dining room will have to be completely done over to hide gouging made where electric wires were put in after work had been completed. 16. Ditto billiard room walls marked from same method of procedure. 17. Upper hall walls spoiled for same reason." Outside the billiard room in the courtyard there was a "regular fish pond" every time it rained! Doors and windows leaked and water ran down into the rooms below and the dining room was constantly flooded. He had no hot water in his bathroom. He writes at length on "botched" cedar woodwork complaining, "Mrs O'Neill and I both relied on your judgment about these details, when we told you we wanted the house kept in the old Bermuda style."

The building of a wing was to be postponed and O'Neill did not want to pay Hill for the plans he had done of it! With some justification Hill was going to "place the matter in my lawyers hands." However, "I shall wait a few days longer before taking this action, hoping to receive your check. Very truly yours Frederick P. Hill."

It was slow going finishing up as materials had to be moved by horse and cart and errands done by a man with a bicycle. All work was done by hand by skilled men (some not so skilled!) measuring, positioning, wielding saws and hammers. Life was simple, unhurried, secluded, removed from contemporary trends in the arts and world events.

In the isolation of Bermuda and his own figurative "two acres of Siberia" O'Neill was doubly removed from the activities of other writers of his day. His pleasure was his work and for that he needed to be by himself. His mind dwelt on the theatre. His friends, whom he liked and needed, were also in the theatrical world. In 1925 there was a great burgeoning of literature on both sides of the Atlantic. Audiences were rejoicing in the plays of Bernard Shaw. (Shaw associated O'Neill as being steamed up with alcohol and when he heard the playwright had given it up he said, "He'll probably never write a good play again"). Yeats and Joyce were bringing prestige to Irish letters. Everybody was reading Galsworthy's *Forsyte Saga*. (He would win a Nobel Prize.) On a lighter note Noel Coward was launched on his great popularity with *The Constant Nymph*. (He would later buy part of the Spithead estate.) In the French capital young American intellectuals were making their mark. Ernest Hemingway would describe the youthful antics of those now famous people, Gertrude Stein, Ezra Pound, the Fitzgeralds, Ford Madox Ford and others, in his entertaining book *A Moveable Feast: Sketches of the Author's Life in Paris in the Twenties*. If O'Neill knew of this community of American writers overseas he would not have wanted to join them. Isolation was his need.

Harbour Rd.
J Waters

Chapter 7

Agnes' father dies. Shane enters a Bermudian school. Renovations at
Spithead continue.
The playwright is emotionally adrift, trying to love two women at once.

At Spithead the great play *Strange Interlude* progressed day by day,
O'Neill recording he wrote twenty-seven days during January. He
reviewed the first four acts of the long piece before proceeding with the
next five. One critic described it as "more Freudian soap opera than
classical tragedy." The subject matter of the play created furore, and
predictably, the work was banned in Boston because it dealt with
"abortion, adultery and homosexuality."

In choosing names for the characters, O'Neill thought of two friends,
Charles Demuth and Marsden Hartley whom he had met long ago in
the "Hell Hole" in Greenwich Village, a haunt of seafarers and intellectuals. The two men were artists and Demuth, whose work is now in the
Metropolitan Museum of Art, painted a picture of the famous pub's
interior. For *Strange Interlude,* O'Neill combined the names of the two
men into Charles Marsden for one of the characters with homosexual

tendencies. Demuth and Marsden painted in St. George's, the old capital of Bermuda, in 1917 and perhaps it was from their enthusiastic accounts of the island that O'Neill first became interested in trying it as a retreat.

Another character in the play is named Darrell. O'Neill may have taken the name from the Bermuda Darrells who lived nearby along Harbour Road. They were a seafaring family, landowners, boat builders and yachtsmen. A sibling, Josephine, was a playmate of Oona. For another character, a young girl, O'Neill chose Madeline, the name of one of the daughters of his friend W.B. Smith.

Strange Interlude is the story of Nina, the daughter of a professor, whose youthful love is shattered by the death in action of her beloved Gordon, an aviator. She leaves her home in a New England town to nurse the returning war wounded. Through some convoluted thinking, she compensates the patients for their wartime horrors by fornicating rather freely with some of them. In the hospital she meets Dr. Darrell, who will play a large part in her life along with the other two men who love her. One, Marsden, is an intellectual mother's boy who lives near her home and who adores her. The other man is Evans a straightforward young fellow whom Nina, urged by Darrell, marries. When Nina becomes pregnant, her mother-in-law tells her of the history of insanity in the family and Nina decides to have an abortion. Evans desperately wants a child. Nina and Darrell decide that he should father a child for her on a strictly biological level. They fall in love and their affair goes much beyond the scientific. The child is a boy christened Gordon. Both Nina and Evans, who suspects nothing, lavish love on and are proud of the fine child. Darrell finally extricates himself from Nina's cloying passions by departing for Europe, where he stays for several years, resuming his real scientific research eventually in the tropics. Nina settles down to family life. Marsden visits when he is not writing his books, which have never been much of a success, or looking after his mother who is now an elderly invalid. Evans dies of a stroke and the drama of feelings in Marsden and Darrell, who has just returned from abroad, erupts. Young Gordon moves far away with the charming Madeline he is about to marry. Nina will lose her second Gordon. The stage directions state: "Resignation has come into her [Nina's] face, a resignation that uses no make-up, that has given up the struggle to be sexually attractive and look younger." She turns to Marsden. Darrell persuades her to ask Marsden to marry her, which she agrees to do.

Darrell will return to his "cells-sensible unicellular life that floats in the sea and has never learned the cry for happiness!" In the end Nina exclaims, "Strange Interlude! Yes, our lives merely are strange dark interludes in the electrical display of God the Father!"

Critics see in this play O'Neill's guilt over his relationship with Carlotta and see in Darrell his own image, described in the play directions: "His dark eyes. His head is handsome and intelligent. There is a quality about him provoking and disturbing to women." Many phrases spoken by Darrell are attributed to O'Neill's own romantic feelings: "...touch of her skin! ...her nakedness! ...What do I care for anything else? ...I've got to break with her!... bad enough now!... but to go on with it!... what a mess it'd make of all our lives!"

At Spithead the blustery days of February alternated with the stillness of a glassy calm when a Bermuda High stood over the island. Then the sun would blaze warmly all day and the tourists would go to the beach. Spithead like all Bermuda houses had no central heating so when the temperatures dropped into the fifties in the evenings, a big fire in one of the huge chimney pieces cheered the family and rubber hot water bottles in their beds warmed the clammy sheets. During the day everyone wore woolens. (It was the English pattern of living. Winston Churchill once remarked that heating in English houses had stood still for centuries since Roman times when heating was done with many hot water channels under the floors.) At Spithead on winter nights sleep would be disturbed when glittering electrical storms swept in off the Atlantic. Great clashes of thunder reverberated over the sea crashing above the big roof, rumbling off to the distant islands. The brilliant flashes of lightening illuminated the sky like day. All creatures' hearts trembled at the power of nature. Dogs crawled under the beds and cats could not be found.

In the great push to finish the long play, O'Neill had not written to Carlotta for some time. He writes, "I've been meaning to write to you for the past week but I've honestly been slaving so hard on *Strange Interlude* - working from eight-thirty in the morning until three or four in the afternoon, staying in bed and having my breakfast and lunch sent up to me to insure against disturbing interruptions - that for the remainder of the day, I've felt too dull-witted to attempt anything beyond browsing around in books". He describes black periods and groaning with despair when he thinks he may not have succeeded in conveying what he wants to say in the play. He says "When it is done

—and by this I mean even the first draft of it—I shall emit a frantic shriek of joy and deliverance...."

Bolly Powell often took the O'Neills sailing in *Flirt* and his wife cared for them in the bad days ahead. *(Bermudian Magazine)*

Lawrence Langner, for many years influential in the Theatre Guild, arrived in Bermuda in mid-March on board the S.S. *Veendam*, which was on the first leg of a West Indian cruise. He had paid $75 for his ticket on the outward passage and would return by a different ship. The purpose of his visit was two fold, partly to restore his health and partly to satisfy his curiosity about what O'Neill was writing. He had known the playwright since the days of his early plays which the Guild turned down. O'Neill's reputation was ever rising and it was time the Guild took another look. The dramatist invited him to Spithead and gave him the first six acts (the last three were not typed) of *Interlude* to read and records: "L. likes *Interlude*." The meeting was significant because the Guild had never produced a play by O'Neill. Langner had one of the exciting new home movie cameras and took pictures of the family and Spithead.

O'Neill was never very satisfied with photographs taken of himself but a steward on one of the ships took pictures of him he thought were more the "real me". The Bermuda Trade Development Board persuaded him to pose for photographs they would use in tourist advertisements in the *New York Times* and other papers. He wrote to Carlotta that they made him look glum. "They were taken more or less under duress. Such is the fate of one so notorious as to become an advertising medium! But it has its compensations. The steamship people are extra obliging in their rates to us -" A picture that was taken later on, he wrote made him look like a "decayed fish"!

O'Neill was often sombre and, according to George Powell, who worked on the seawall, "a very serious man-as though he was carrying the weight of a nation. If any of us said, 'Mr. O'Neill?' he would merely grunt except to my father, he talked freely to him."

Harold and Helen DePolo, old friends of the O'Neills, had taken a house in Bermuda. DePolo, who was a short story and article writer, had at one time given O'Neill's brother Jamie a home when he had nowhere to go. Recently the DePolos, who had a house in Maine, had visited at Loon Lodge and Harold who was a keen fisherman persuaded the O'Neills to go on a short fishing expedition in the White Mountains. The two men had a long association going back to the Provincetown days where they were involved in what they probably later thought of as a humorous event but at the time was anything but. They were arrested by the F.B.I.! They liked to walk on the dunes and beaches where the wind blew in off the great Atlantic and a lighthouse and radio station stood on rocky promontories. At the time, 1917 during the Great War, spy hunts were the order of the day for the F.B.I. and authors were watched because they were thought to have unorthodox or radical views. Unfortunately the two men came under scrutiny when a young policeman thought he saw them taking an interest in the radio station and flashing a signal out to sea presumably to a German submarine! The instrument turned out to be a typewriter glinting in the sun! They were jailed overnight but no charge was ever brought. However, the memorandum F.B.I. file 61-52-96 remained on record and was not declassified until 1982, almost sixty years later.

Agnes suggested to Helen that they rent Southcote, where Oona was born or the Trott house on the south shore but Helen feared the houses were too isolated. Her husband was a heavy drinker and she liked him to have plenty to do. They rented in the charming community of Salt Kettle where the ferry ran over to Hamilton. They would be along the Paget shore not far from Spithead. (The kettle for boiling sea water to make salt had long since disappeared and salt was no longer made on the island.)

One spring day when Granaway Deep, without a ripple, was a shimmering slate drawn over with softly undulating clouds and reflections of boats and islands in reverse, a young Bermudian artist, Hereward Watlington, bicycled over to Spithead with a friend.

"My friend thought O'Neill was a god!" Hereward remembered. "He persuaded me to go with him to see if his idol would let me paint his portrait. I was just back from Paris where I had been a pupil of Andre Dohti, the cubist painter. We were politely received at Spithead. There seemed to be fire burning in O'Neill's eyes", the artist reflected, "they were fiery brown—beautiful eyes. Agnes looked like a Burne Jones type of person." The young painter was fresh from the influence of Dohti who gave so much of his time to youth in his now famous school and who made a cult of Cezanne. Agnes and O'Neill were very cordial to the young artist and his friend. The dramatist said he was immersed in writing a play and would not have time to sit.

The year before George Bellows had written to O'Neill saying he would like to paint his portrait. He was a friend from the old waterfront days at Jimmy the Priest's. Unfortunately Bellows died suddenly before O'Neill could answer his letter.

In April the *Royal Gazette and Colonist Daily* announced that "Mrs. Eugene O'Neill, wife of the famous playwright left on the *Fort Victoria* for New York." News had come that Agnes's father, Edward Boulton, was dying of tuberculosis in a sanatorium in Connecticut, so she was hastening north. When O'Neill returned home to Spithead after seeing the boat off he went into the depths of despondency. In a nervous turmoil he went all to pieces. "God how I miss you! I actually broke down on the bed in our room in a fit of hysterical crying when I first went up there. I know it is a bit absurd, but my whole control seems gone...*I need you, need you, need you!* intensely more now than ever before in our married life." He continues his lament, "I'm just alone and miserable, and will be until your return. Because I love you!... I kiss your dear lips and body. Your lover always Gene."

The next night he wrote, "My Own Aggie: Well, I've certainly been feeling lost since that moment when your dear familiar beautiful face blurred out into the background of the receding *Fort Victoria* and I about faced and took up my burden of a wifeless life for a spell.... I drove right back to *Our Home*. Our Home! I feel that very much about Spithead, don't you? That this place is in some strange symbolic fashion our reward, that it is the permanent seat of our family—like some old English family estate. I already feel like entailing it in my will so that it must always be background for our children! I love Spithead—and not with my old jealous, bitter possessiveness—my old man Cabotism!— but as ours, not mine except as mine is included in ours. The thought of the place is indissolubly intermingled with my love for you, with our nine years of marriage that, after much struggle, have finally won to this haven, this ultimate island where we may rest and live toward our dreams with a sense of permanence and security that here we do belong."

He assures Agnes that he has told her the truth about Carlotta, that it was only a "gesture of a Virginal Casanova" and that she should forgive him even as she would forgive Shane if he were to kiss Peggy Anne! He had been swimming, practicing his tennis strokes and had played with Oona who was in "fine shape." He had allowed Shane to go to the movie matinee in Hamilton of *Rin Tin Tin* with Peggy Anne and the Huber's nurse. In ending his letter he declared, "I love you so damned much! We must get away alone to the beaches and places when you return. We don't do enough of that. We ought to have our private life together as well as our life in our family. Kisses and kisses, Dear!" The next day was Easter Sunday and O'Neill wrote what fun Oona and Shane had looking for Easter eggs hidden by Gaga about the garden. They were very low in water, the tank almost empty. Simons and Johnston could hardly scoop any with buckets on ropes, and he would have to order some. Henry Watlington (later Sir Henry) had found a large lens of underground water and had formed the Watlington Water

O'Neill in a kayak at Spithead with a loving message for Carlotta written on the bow. (*Yale University*)

Works providing the only source of water in the island other than collected rain. However, the horse-drawn tank-wagon was of necessity, small as a horse could only pull so much, and several loads would only amount to a few inches in the bottom of the huge Spithead tank. It was expensive. Running out of water was considered a near disaster. In times of drought prayers for rain were said in the churches and the skies were constantly searched for black clouds. He assured Agnes that DePolo had not turned up at the house. Agnes had feared he might tempt O'Neill to go on a binge. He closes tenderly, "Again all my love, Own Sweetheart! I can't tell you how much I long for you to be here again! Kisses! Gene."

O'Neill was temperamentally adrift and it was not until Agnes came back that he was able to go back to work. Then his thoughts turned to a new play *Dynamo* and he wrote, "It is really the first play of a trilogy that will dig at the roots of the sickness of to-day as I feel it—the death of an old God and the failure of science and materialism to give any satisfying new one.... It seems to me that anyone trying to do big work nowadays must have this big subject behind all the little subjects of his plays or novels, or he is simply scribbling around on the surface of things. O'Neill had seen a dynamo at a hydro-electrical plant near Ridgefield that generated electricity from the waters of New England rivers. In the play the enormous generator "is huge and black, with something of a great massive ebony idol about it."

Gratifying news came at the end of April, by cable, from the Theatre Guild saying they would take *Marco Millions* , an option on *Strange Interlude* and an option on three other plays. It could turn into a prestigious opportunity in production and an assurance of an income, the latter badly needed. He decided to go to New York for discussions and left in May, sailing on Oona's second birthday. He wrote to Agnes on the voyage "I have been teetering on the verge of sea-sickness ever since we lost Bermuda under the horizon, and it hasn't been so terribly rough at that. What a hell of an admission for an old windjammer sailor, what!" He reassures Agnes, "Dearest, I love you and I don't love anyone else and that's all there is to it! Again all love and good-night, sweetest. Kiss the heirs for me. I'll cable when there's any news. Gene."

Carlotta was in New York, spring was in the air and O'Neill saw her nearly every day. Louis Sheaffer describing the visit to the city does not mention Carlotta but the playwright notes in his diary the many occasions on which they met. O'Neill was staying with the Langners who persuaded him to let them give a small party for him. He was introduced to a critic, Joseph Wood Krutch. Louis Sheaffer writes, "Apparently Eugene, who took a quick liking to the critic, wanted to counter the popular view of himself as a gloomy forbidding figure with the air of a "somewhat naughty boy" O'Neill told Krutch that sometimes when he was drunk in Bermuda he used to strip off all his clothes and, with a hibiscus tucked behind his ear, run along the beach in the moonlight reciting his own verse.

From New York in dramatic words O'Neill wrote to Agnes: "I love you. For over nine years I have loved you and you alone, loved you with my whole being, without reservation given you my whole life. I seem to hear a single doubt, an exception a sorrowful suspicion creeping into your mind to destroy its peace. You will think of Carlotta. Don't! Dear one! Please! If you could only look into my heart and mind and see how little trace is left there.... One hair of your head is more to me than the whole body and soul, liver and lights, of any other woman!"

Upon his return home, O'Neill found the sea a perfect temperature. Bermudians had just enjoyed the holiday of Empire Day, the twenty-fourth of May, celebrated around the British world, and had taken their first swims of the year. Although some swam all the year round it was a local joke that the twenty-fourth started the swimming season. O'Neill had an inflatable raft and he liked to drift with the incoming tide a mile down to Salt Kettle. He was "hail fellow well met" with many salt-air characters who plied for hire in rowing and sailing boats, even motor boats, around the Inverurie Hotel and one of them would often tow him back home against the tide or if no one was about, Powell says, he would carry the raft home along Harbour Road.

His affinity for the sea had been with him since his youth. He had intended, years ago, to write a play about himself calling it "The Sea Mother's Son." The play was never written but the title was sometimes used to describe him. He said the sub-title of the play would be "The Story of the Birth of a Soul." Louis Sheaffer writes, "...the idea of developing a 'Soul' was constantly in his thoughts." When drifting on the raft O'Neill was under the great blue dome of the heavens overhead and all around in the sky the huge white thunder-head clouds of summer billowed higher and higher like the clouds in old paintings where God sat in judgement. Sometimes around three o'clock in the afternoon a tissue of clouds formed above the island looking like a great sprawling figure of a man up in the sky. Bermudians say he is Morgan the pirate looking down on what he never captured.

O'Neill continued with *Dynamo* at the end of May but soon set it aside. The fate of *Strange Interlude* still hung in the balance. He spent weeks going over the whole play again, all nine acts until he was as satisfied as he ever could be. *Lazarus Laughed,* mostly written at Bellevue, was to be published. He took much trouble over the final draft of this cherished play. His prediction had proved right so far that no one would ever produce the play because the elaborate scenes, the masks, the crowds and the music would make it prohibitively expensive. He wanted to write a special introduction for the book, setting forth "all my long-cherished ideas and ideals about the theatre." He had so many ideas on the subject they simply would not fit into an introduction. He was pressed with anxieties, quarrelling with Agnes and feeling the heat. The introduction was a big disappointment, he wrote, "no... needs a book which I ought to write some time."

Agnes herself was experiencing difficult times. In spite of all O'Neill's reassurances about his love for her and his home, and the unimportance of Carlotta to him she felt unsteady. The fun and joy of the renovations of their hoped for perfect-home-at-last, which O'Neill delegated to her, had an overcast of doubts. He *needed* her, she knew. But did he need her quite so completely as he had during the old drunken years? Their relationship was not the same and she would have to adjust to the new O'Neill. She had never had so much spare time with plenty of servants, Gaga and a nursemaid. She was not one to join in local activities as so many American residents did, giving of their time and talents to the island's charities. Perhaps it was the isolation of Spithead which cut her off from local society. Certainly O'Neill's anti-social attitude did not make for new friends. She had abandoned her writing. Her husband was absorbed in his play and liked to sail with his acquaintances for relaxation. Paradoxically it was Agnes who was enjoying a few drinks at this time. O'Neill blamed the Hubers, with some justification. Their butler, Timony, says she often came over to join her amusing neighbours for a drink. He would give her a bottle to take home. O'Neill did not want liquor in the house, understandably. It was a source of bitterness to him who still smoked but never drank.

O'Neill's mind raced ahead with new ideas for plays, among them a "new Negro play". Years before he had written a play *All God's Chillun Got Wings* dealing with the love of a young coloured man for a white girl in a depressed area of a big American city. At Spithead he was surrounded by coloured people and saw their position in Bermudian society. Poor education kept many a clever coloured man at the artisan level and many a woman in the kitchen or at the sewing machine. The small island had no university so higher education was sought overseas. There were two coloured doctors, a few teachers and lawyers but on the whole artisan and menial jobs were the lot of the coloured people. Discrimination went unchecked in offices and shops. As to the law, it applied to all fair and square in this British territory. In politics there were two coloured elected members of the House of Assembly, the governing body of Bermuda. O'Neill never wrote the play. His thoughts on the play were never revealed; it was never clear if he was thinking of the African in the New World or in his native land.

The family was spending the summer in Bermuda, as O'Neill wanted to see if they could use the house all year round. Also, the renovations needed supervision and were costing more than expected so money was short. The Hubers had gone home to America and many Bermudians had sailed on the ships that plied directly to England for the summer. The voyage took two weeks, as stops were made in Spain and France. The businessman's trips and vacations to Europe involved a month's snoozing in deck chairs no matter which way he went.

Unfortunately, O'Neill caught flu, which was very hard to shake off in the hot weather. "I have been feeling like the wrath of Christ for the past ten days laid up with tonsils, sore throat, cough, cold in the head and all the fixings. It has meant keeping out of the briny and that has peeved me no end." Some days he could not work and that peeved him too. In the 1920's there was no escape to air-conditioning and a little breeze from a small electrical fan was the most that could be done to dispel the hot air on a still night. The tree toads peeped until dawn. Wire netting was a great invention and the houses were screened against flies and mosquitoes. However, the inevitable mosquito crept in to torment the tossing invalid.

It took O'Neill weeks to get better. He wrote "I'm pretty pepless yet, but it may be the climate, which is 85-90 night and day without let up. You get so you pray for a good old grey New England day murky 24 hours.... The climate has sort of got me licked temporarily but Aggie and the kids eat it up."

Carlotta, who was uncertain of seeing O'Neill, went off to Europe for the summer to take the waters at a German spa. He wrote a lackluster letter telling her about his flu and cough, the heat, the boredom, how the sea was too warm and on and on. He blamed his miseries on his inability to be with her. He begged her not to forget him. He ends, "Or, for your sake, please do! Good-bye for this time, dear. All love, Carlotta. Gene."

Young Josephine Darrell, aged five, had a French governess who was friendly with Gaga and she enjoyed taking the little girl to Spithead to play with Oona. Josephine says she and Oona would peep quietly over a garden wall to watch O'Neill doing his exercises on a lawn or writing out of doors. Speaking of her own home she remembers it "as a warm, wonderful place where we all had fun together. At the O'Neills there was not the same feeling."

Patty and Jimmy Light, newly married, came to stay for several weeks. "That has been a bit of a treat," wrote O'Neill, "and relaxation for me, having him to talk to. Jimmy is one of my oldest friends and he has one of the few imaginative minds connected with the theatre." Eugene, Jr. who was now six feet tall also came to stay. O'Neill had recently written, "I find him a son I can well take a paternal pride in. He is my sort." The large household was expensive. Much of O'Neill's inheritance was being poured into Spithead and the Ridgefield house had not sold. He was dependent on royalties and at this time not much was coming in, although the future looked bright. Some of the many guests that summer would later gossip about the household and the tension they said they felt there. For amusement the O'Neills took them to the south shore beaches for evening picnics as the sun was going down and the prevailing southerly winds lowered the temperature to almost chilly. As it grew dark shooting stars streaked across the heavens and Orion's belt and dagger sparkled in the vast dark sky. In that unusually hot summer the early morning or late afternoon were the times to use the tennis court. The sail boat, the clinker built skiff, the kayak, the raft, the diving board all provided amusement and Shane was especially happy. He was often lonely and enjoyed the visitors who had time to take an interest in him and his fishing. Oona ran about followed faithfully by Hilda who made sure the two year old did not topple overboard.

Bermudians loved camping so tents bloomed on the cliffs where families settled for a month or more. Some of the well-to-do moved to their bungalows on the small islands where their children learnt to handle boats and become strong swimmers. The Boy Scouts and Girl Guides went into camp. It was against the law to join islands together or to the mainland so the bays, sounds and harbours remained peaceful settings for outings. Past Spithead went the pleasure boats hired by Lodges or Societies to take their members to the islands, often with bands on board. From the boats came the sound of singing to the music of banjoes or guitars. (No thumping amplified music in those days.)

When the visitors were gone, O'Neill was stressed, angry and run down at the end of August, and was quarrelling with Agnes. He felt he must go to New York and firm up matters with the Guild and even expected rehearsals might start. Being alone was something he could not stand and he urged Agnes to go with him. The lack of money was serious. Her city clothes were out of date and worn and the children had outgrown everything. As Brook Farm in Ridgefield had not sold he tried to persuade her to move the household there in spite of sparse furnishings.

After much discussion, with funds so low, it was decided O'Neill should go to New York alone. They spent the evening before he sailed in loving romance on the wharf under the tropical sky. From the *Fort St. George* he sent Agnes a marconigram with a hidden message she was supposed to decipher. In a letter he explains he meant: "Remember our front of house steamer chair love: I wanted you to have pleasant loving thoughts of me my first night away as you remembered the night before. Did you blush when it came to you over the phone?"

In the next paragraph he tells her how he wishes "so longingly that you were with me!" He feels everything is "right now after the nervous bickerings and misunderstandings of the summer." He is sure their love for each other will endure for the rest of their lives, the bitterness gone. He is so lonely without her but it will not be long before he comes back or she goes north. "And I feel when we see each other again we will love as never before!"

O'Neill arrived in New York to find everyone he wanted to see out of town. Carlotta was still in Europe. His small hotel room was stiflingly hot, the window catching little breeze in the canyons of the tall buildings. From there he wrote dramatic letters almost as though he were a character in one of his own plays. His tiny handwriting boiled with strong emotions, indulging in self-pity and heaping blame on Agnes. He wrote to her: "It is not good to force me to be lonely and homeless under most unfortunate conditions when I'm sick in the bargain. You have thought of yourself and the inconvenience moving the kids would cause you but you have not considered me or my work—or even my health. All my love! I miss you like the devil or I wouldn't mind all this so much. You must realize this! Not that my love or loneliness can mean much to you, judging by the way you've arranged this all-important fall season for me! By the time rehearsals start I ought to be a fine morbid wreck."

When the bills for summer entertaining came Agnes wrote to O'Neill accounting for expenses which were much more than budgeted. The drug store bill! Jimmy and Patty Light had charged on the O'Neill account and Eugene Jr. aged seventeen smoked and cigarettes cost $1.80 a carton. Beer and ale cost 25 cents a bottle. They had had liquor in the house and had enjoyed some Benedictine. The Lights had run out of money, only having $6 left for the days on board ship, going back, and arriving in New York. She had lent them $25. She knew they would repay everything.

There was something almost masochistic in the way Agnes skimped on her household spending. All through the years they were married she managed what money they had carefully. Her letters to O'Neill tell him about household expenses in detail, obviously wanting him to admire her self-sacrifice and appreciate her good management. He, on the other hand, rarely mentions money and never comments on her efforts. His biographers imply he was stingy and it was plain Agnes rarely joined him during his trips to New York. It seems as though he invited her, knowing she would be practical and not come. With two children and a nurse it certainly was expensive to travel and Agnes rarely left the children. In Bermuda her wardrobe had run down. Ready-to-wear clothes in the shops were frumpy and although dress-makers on the island were skilled, dresses came out looking a bit homemade. Elegance was hard to attain.

Agnes also wrote chatty letters. She referred to how O'Neill had kissed Gaga good-bye when he left. Gaga boasted to Lily that O'Neill had called her a "Wenus" (Bermudian for Venus). Lily and Hilda went into hilarious fits of laughter thinking of Gaga as a Wenus. The coloured people used some Elizabethan English in their speech and pronounced *vs* as *ws* and "wice wersa." Instead of Mrs. they would call Agnes Mistress O'Neill. (An indignant English lady when called Mistress So-and-So protested severely, "I am not his *mistress* I am his *wife!*")

Oona suffered from the heat and broke out with boils that would not heal, a common ailment for children at the end of summer in those days. Too much salt water local people said was the cause. Gaga got them too.

During the hot months people became run down and fresh produce arriving by ship was expensive and not so fresh at that. Locally there were bananas, pumpkins (West Indian variety), christopheens, and pawpaws, which could be cooked when green as a vegetable or eaten as a fruit when ripe. Sweet potatoes were plentiful, but green vegetables and salad ingredients (except for cucumbers and sweet peppers) would not grow. Vitamin supplements were unheard of.

Agnes was worried and wrote to O'Neill that she was taking Oona to see Dr. Tucker as he was known to be good with children. She thought the Bermudian attitude towards boils was too casual. The doctor, who had delivered Oona in 1925 and had driven O'Neill in his buggy, had his office hours in rooms at the back of his home from two to four o'clock. Every afternoon at four o'clock tea was served in the dining room at Park House, where a welcome awaited friends. The hot scones are remembered to this day. Patients who were known socially were sometimes invited in. Mrs. Tucker, a busy woman, who campaigned for women's suffrage and public clinics for children, presided over the silver tea service. (She was undaunted when The Women's Suffrage Bill had been recently defeated in the House of Assembly by twenty-five to nine.) Park House was right in town on the corner of Victoria Street and Cedar Avenue with stables at the back. The Tuckers were intensely British, so the children attended schools and colleges in England and the Union Jack flew daily from the upper verandah.

Agnes was furious about the boils and raged against Bermudians who she thought refused to admit there were any or to do anything about them because they did not wish to give their island a bad name.

> (Note. Dr. Simon Frazer, retired Chief Medical Officer, says the deep painful sores called boils are caused by staphylococcus bacteria which breed in moisture on the skin, particularly in hot weather. They are not seen as often today, he believes, because antibiotics are killing off so many bacteria, and incidentally opening the way for more viral infections.)

From New York, O'Neill went to stay with friends in Redding, Connecticut, and visited the house in Ridgefield, referring to it in a letter to Agnes as "our home." Agnes wrote she was comforted by the reference to Brook Farm which he often abused. He asked her again to open the house and bring the children up. For the second time she refused to do it. This would rankle with her husband and would bubble to the top during his simmering emotional stewings. Again it was a question of money. O'Neill worried intensely in case *Marco Millions* was a failure, "and *Interlude* doesn't go on (if the Guild passes it, this is possible) Hopkins won't do it and Liveright is only talking big." As he stayed on in New York, sadly, bitter sniping started in their correspondence and the earlier loving tone seemed to fade. He wrote, in despair that he could not do without drinking and without love. Agnes made no move to close down the work at Spithead, temporarily, and move back to Brook Farm.

O'Neill tarried in New York. He had no further theatre business to do as the Guild had signed. *Marco Millions* and *Strange Interlude* would be produced but not until the following January and it was much too soon for rehearsals. They would not advance any money. He had been consulting doctors who found he had a low thyroid count. It would take some time before the correct dose could be determined to bring his thyroid back to normal.

Carlotta had returned from Europe and O'Neill saw her frequently. They drove out to Danbury where he wanted to see the Hydro Electric Power Station, once more, the inspiration for *Dynamo*. As the season advanced in the city, O'Neill began a life of high sophistication that contrasted with the boredom of Agnes's existence. The theatre world was in its busy autumn season, and he met many celebrities—indeed he was one himself—and was entertained by those he already knew. O'Neill wrote to Agnes about a visit to Maurice Wertheim, stockbroker and director of the Theatre Guild. "I was up at Wertheim's for dinner one night, met Stieglitz and Georgia O'Keefe there and liked them immensely." (Years later, in Bermuda, Georgia O'Keefe made her famous drawings of the banana in bud which are now in the Museum of Modern Art in New York City.) O'Neill saw, that autumn, the new Broadway productions. The beautiful Carlotta hung on his arm at many events.

After O'Neill had been gone nearly a month Agnes wrote she had decided to go up. He replied, "Darling I do wish you were here! But don't come!" He would be home in two weeks so it wasn't worth it. Only the week before in a vicious letter he had accused her because she did not come to him: "There's no reason I can figure out except that you must have a lover down there as I suspected before!" The tirade went on: "You know damn well I'm not interested in little sex affairs for sex's sake alone, that it is love or nothing! Do you want me to love someone else? Oh hell again! What sort of game is this you're playing, Agnes?" Receiving this, Agnes was hurt and furious. Between the boat mails bitter feelings lingered, then the apology came, "Forgive that crazy letter and forget it, please do! Remember we both want to start a new life together." A few days later: "Sweetheart, I do long for you so much these days! Now that the time is growing shorter and I know I'll see you in two weeks, I'm simply eaten up by impatience and actually counting the days! How's that for a nine years husband amid the wiles and glamours of N.Y.? I think I'm pretty close to being a model! It will be so marvellous to take you in my arms and kiss you again! As I write this an image of your beautiful face comes close to mine and I seem to feel and smell your body touching mine and I get goose flesh all over - not to mention other things which I won't make you blush by mentioning!... Not so long now, Darling - (but much too long!) - and then-!... Your lover, Gene."

The weeks dragged for Agnes, as O'Neill did not return in the promised two weeks. Many of their acquaintances were abroad, and she was isolated with the children, Gaga, the servants, and workmen. George Powell says Agnes "had her ways" but was very nice to the people on Cedar Hill. She had a picnic for the children from up there, getting Lily to prepare the food. Her spirits were raised, in the hot September weather, when someone lent her a horse and carriage to take care of for a month. She was fearful O'Neill would be angry with her and sent him a detailed account of what it cost to feed a horse, contrasted with the savings there would be. The ferry being over a mile away they were accustomed to hiring a hack to take them there and back. She could also sometimes take the children to the south shore. The horse was not too lively to drive and Scott was taking care of him. Still fearful of her husband's anger she promised to return the horse when he came home.

At Spithead an eighteenth century feature was the large fish pond on the wharf. In the days before refrigeration it was a place to put fish from a large catch, to keep them alive, assuring a supply of fresh fish for the household. Even in 1926 the art of freezing food was hardly thought of so the pond was still useful as well as ornamental. Swimming and gliding about in the deep pond were blue and gold angel fish, scarlet, big eyed, squirrel fish, striped sargent majors, "yaller" grunts and other wonders of the tropical sea. Sometimes towards dusk a fisherman would stop by on his way in from the ocean to sell a few crayfish to keep in the pond for a special occasion. Then Lily would make a cold lobster salad or a hot Newburg served with rice.

Shane had become something of an expert little fisherman. The workmen taught him how to bait up for different kinds of fish inhabiting the sparkling water. Sometimes a huge shark was sighted cruising on the surface above the gloomy waters of Granaway Deep. Ships threw garbage overboard in those days, inshore, and sharks followed these ships through the reefs feeding on leftovers, coming even into Hamilton Harbour. One afternoon Shane caught a large porgy and a ten pound shark! People rushed to his assistance when he hooked the shark to keep him from being pulled into the sea by the big fish. He had his picture taken with the shark to send to his father who regrettably was not there to praise the little boy. However he did write a warm, affectionate letter to Shane, calling him the best fisherman in the family. Bermudian cooks made a delicious shark dish with hot peppers using the huge livers from the fish. It was a great favorite with the men as it was considered an aphrodisiac. O'Neill wrote that he always wanted to taste shark.

Life at Spithead was bucolic, and Agnes entered into the spirit of the late September season when it was time to plough the fields. She supervised the planting of potatoes and vegetable seeds. On the home farm the chickens, Rhode Island Reds, provided a supply of fresh eggs for the house. Shane became very fond of the chickens. The silky feathers of the hens were nice to stroke and the tail feathers from the saucy rooster were "collectibles" for the seven-year-old. The two sons of the handsome foreman, Johnson, were Shane's companions.

Sometimes at night Agnes would write O'Neill wild letters in reply to his snide suggestions that she had a lover. Perhaps he was easing his own conscience. The dreadful exchange of letters continued. "Kind" friends wrote to Agnes about her husband's life in New York which drove her to further unhappiness. O'Neill worried about hurricanes and wrote that if the children were harmed he would never forgive her. Carlotta's elegance swam before her eyes as she wrote that she could not go to New York as she and the children had only old clothes. The gift he said he had sent her had not arrived.

The present was a travelling dressing case, much in fashion. No lady travelling in those days felt she was from the upper crust without one. It was a leather case fitted with a silver backed brush and comb, silver topped crystal bottles and jars for lotions and creams, a compartment for nail scissors, files and a lemon stick, and a silver backed pad for buffing nails. (No nail polish then.) O'Neill had had the silver tops engraved with her initials.

Finally in a crescendo of despair she wrote that the money had run out for renovations, she never saw anyone, she had no more interest in the garden and if she had not mislaid her key she would have taken out her little pistol, gone out in a boat and finished it.

Autumn days in New York were turning cold. O'Neill had been away for the best part of two months. He needed to get home for he was unsure where life was leading him. He had eased his conscience with accusations and acrimony in letters to Agnes but this did not mean he had no feelings for her, the children, or his new estate and secluded way of living in Bermuda. His health problems settled, he sailed for home late in October. Of the city, he wrote, "(it) rattles the old bean of one grown used to Bermuda bicycles and hacks." He had done no creative work for weeks and the work habit of years was calling him, too.

Once again the slow pace and quiet of the island cast a spell over O'Neill. The water temperature was seventy-five degrees and he threw himself into the sea and allowed the complexities of New York and his involvements slip away in the refreshing salty water. Work was still going on about the place but was much reduced. Everyone was reminded about O'Neill's own private strip of grass on the point where he did his exercises. No one was allowed there.

To Kenneth Macgowan, his trusted friend, O'Neill sent a check and note, "With the one will you purchase flowers - roses - or use your own judgement or the florist's as to what would be best - I don't know flower lingo - and send to Carlotta.... Many thanks!... I need a little of the glue of God, I'm afraid - a bit broken. See you soon. Gene." To the lady herself he penned, "God how I long for you!... I am getting all brown again. I lie in the sun and dream of you in the warm air - your warmth. 'Where her last kiss still warms the air' - that is true, Lucidé - air of my life warmed to new life by your sweetness and beauty! Kisses, Shadow Eyes! As always, Gene."

O'Neill started writing the day after he arrived. He was working on a play he had thought of way back at Belgrade Lakes, "a fantastic whimsical play, *Squarehead Saga*." He decided to write the scenario with a moving picture in mind. His thoughts also dwelt on the two plays the Theatre Guild had agreed to produce, *Macro Millions* and *Strange Interlude*. Casting for the new productions was about to start in New York and rehearsals would begin in December. Two major plays in rehearsal at the same time! A publication of *Lazarus Laughed* had come out, and a special edition of *The Emperor Jones* was on the press. The books of his plays were selling in England and had been translated into many languages. Money problems looked as if they would ease up soon. He was exhilarated by the success of his works, emotionally wrought up by his feelings for Carlotta, and torn with guilt over the family he still loved.

O'Neill had been away when the school year started so he and his son had much to talk about. Shane was a day boy at Somers College in the next parish of Southampton. The headmaster was the Reverend Walker, the rector of St. Anne's Church. A rather irascible Church of England clergyman, he ran the school along English lines. The teaching was sound and much emphasis was put on sports. The masters came in their billowing gowns from Oxford, well versed to impart Latin and an appreciation of the classics. Shane dressed in the school uniform, beige cap with badge, white shirt with school tie, beige shorts, beige knee socks and brown shoes. In the cooler weather he would also wear the blue and beige striped blazer. Discipline was strict and the Rev. Walker ever ready to enforce it with his cane. In spite of the decorum required, "old boys" praise the school and smile when they refer to good old times there. Shane is well remembered. A fellow schoolmate said Shane had "plenty of guts." He came out well, if bloody, in a fight with an older bigger boy. It was good that O'Neill was back for Shane's eighth birthday.

Oona, who was recovering from the boils, was two and a half and lived in her small world bounded by her infant routine and the fun and love of all around her. Gaga spoke French to the children and the maids found it beguiling to hear Oona speaking French. Hilda shook her head in near disbelief telling about it. In Hamilton the moving-picture theatre was showing Charlie Chaplin in a *A Dog's Life*. Who could have imagined that the shy little girl at Spithead, would, sixteen years later, become Mrs. Charlie Chaplin?

On October the twenty seventh, O'Neill wrote to Carlotta on Spithead stationery, "Dearest Lady, Evening of Thursday - around six - I'm thinking of you at home before your fire for a spell reading my last mail's letter which should have got to you by this. I hope some of the warm love I felt when I wrote it goes out to you and makes you say again with the adorable half-joyous, half-regretful happy groan 'Oh, you've gone and done it! I love you, damn it!'... I sent you a cable two days ago - just one word 'remember' - oh please do that, Carlotta! ...Remember all

I said that last day! I'll be back soon! November is almost here and the 15th is only two weeks away. I am sure I will be coming up alone. Everything is unchanged. I swim, row, tennis, bike, etc. - feel most husky and healthy - wonderful weather - ...God I'm lonely! When I dream of those hours of ours....Your Gene."

George Powell tells an amazing story concerning Johnson, whom he describes as a fine, big, half-white man. He implies Agnes and Johnson were "very close," even hinting they were lovers. Life had not been easy for Gaga during the long hot summer with mounting tension in the family, O'Neill's long absence, and the tiresome shortage of housekeeping money. She began to spy on Agnes and to imagine some romance was going on, until she felt compelled to go and tell O'Neill. When her husband told her of Gaga's accusations, Agnes flew into a wild rage and Powell says was on the verge of attacking Gaga. Agnes' nerves had been on edge anyway and this betrayal by Gaga, who had been with them so long, was more than Agnes could condone. She ordered Gaga out of the house, packed her up, and put her on the next boat out of the island. O'Neill did not believe what Gaga had said and years later would beg Agnes to make it up with the old nurse in spite of what he refers to as her "idiotic gossip." Lily took over and consoled the children as best she could.

Migratory birds were coming south. Kingfishers had arrived on the property. They came every autumn to make their homes for the winter under the tamarisk trees, which grew along the rocky shore. Sometimes a newly arrived white heron would take up his stationary one-legged vigil on a rock waiting for an unsuspecting fish to come within his range. When the prevailing autumn winds came from the northwest swooping with great gusts over the island they swept many birds, big and small, from the American coast to arrive in the haven of Bermuda. Spithead right on the water was a landing place for many an exhausted traveller.

Storms were swooping too over the owner of Spithead. Strong currents contrary to the birds' direction, were urging him northwards. Great spells of his life had passed in writing or were semi-obliterated for days or even weeks by drunken forgetfulness. The winds of change were blowing hard that autumn. He was in an upward lifting current of literary success and fanned by a gentler zephyr of a love he knew he should not have. He packed a bag and caught a boat. He left his manuscripts and belongings behind, it never occurring to him he would be sailing beyond known horizons. In fact he never was to return.

Spithead
Old Kitchen Cottage
and Privy

J.B.Waters

Chapter 8

The abandoned family struggles to adjust at Spithead.
Finn Mac Cool is murdered.
The playwright is praised for *Marco Millions* and *Strange Interlude* winning
the Pulitzer Prize for the latter.
He elopes with an actress, lives in the South of France, travels to the orient
and is enraged by the divorce delay.

Agnes stood on the dock at Spithead in the cold wind of early December
with O'Neill's letter flapping in her hand. White caps crested the small
waves in Granaway Deep. Deep? The water out there was very deep.
Life's tides were threatening to overwhelm her and she tried to think
how she was going to keep her head above water. She was out to sea
on a foreign island with few friends among Bermudians and none
among the English.

O'Neill's letters at first discussed mutual concerns such as the sale of
the Ridgefield house. He urged her not to make plans for Spithead
beyond those already decided upon. There were debts, and he worried
that the promises of forthcoming productions might never be realized
and they would need a reserve of money on which to live. He added
that now he wanted his manuscripts sent to New York, where he
thought they should be placed in a safety deposit box. "Remember, this
may be a big 'ace in the hole' for us and the kids." He might need to sell

them some day. These were not the words of a husband about to cut and run. Agnes's heart surged up with hope but was quickly dashed down. Although he signed the letter with "Much love" his suggestion that they go their separate ways chilled her deep inside.

Agnes heard from New York that O'Neill had invited people to stay in the New Year at Spithead. She did not know what to think.

Each arriving mail brought torturing letters —how she must be free to do what she wanted, how she was still young and beautiful and could find happiness that she had never had from him. He said he had had none either. She wistfully thought of all the passionate love letters he had written to her that she had kept. Their lives together had been tempestuous at times - fights and loving reconciliations, moods and drunkenness followed by devotion and dependence on each other.

O'Neill asked Agnes if she were coming to New York and hastily added, "I don't mean for the openings." He wallowed in sentiment over Christmas hoping the children would like their presents. "Kiss the children for me," he wrote dramatically. Perhaps he was trying to deal with his guilt by writing "And for their future happiness I am sure it's better for me to be more a friend and less a father than the reverse." Finally a letter arrived telling her that he loved someone else "most deeply" who reciprocated his love. He assured her that she, Agnes, had not loved him for a long time. He offered her Spithead as a permanent home for life.

When they were first married Agnes and O'Neill agreed to part without rancour if either one fell in love with someone else or "until love do us part," as they put it. They were easy words to say. They did not take into account human nature. O'Neill wrote, "There have been moments when our old love flared into life again but you must acknowledge that these have grown steadily rarer. On the other side of the ledger moments of very horrible hate have been more and more apparent, a poisonous bitterness and resentment, a cruel desire to wound, rage and frustration and revenge. This has killed our chance for happiness together. There have been too many insults to pride and self-respect, too many torturing scenes that one may forgive but which something in one cannot forget and which no love, however strong, can continue to endure and live."

He assures Agnes that she will always be able to live in dignity and comfort. He states, "When I say I am happy now, it is deeply true. My only unhappiness is what I expressed in my last letter - a bitter feeling of sadness when I think over all our years together and what the passage of time has done to us." He makes it plain that he wants a divorce. "— it is horrible to face the end of anything one has hugged to one's heart for years—"

At Spithead the wind roared in the huge chimneys and on the smoke from cedarwood fires all the sorrows of the people who had lived in the house took flight for heaven. The ghost of Agnes' prophecy of long ago blew about. She had written to her husband the winter Shane was born about her premonition that when O'Neill became famous and rich something would ruin it for them.

Agnes took ship for New York.

The poignant story of that Christmas at Spithead will long remain in the memories of Bermudians. In the huge house Lily and Dorothy took care of the children. Shane was home for the holidays but the festive season did not seem to be for him quite what his school friends were experiencing. His unhappy mother had left and his father had left too. His home was particularly gloomy in the long dark evenings after Oona had gone to bed. Lily and Dorothy would talk together, while the poor dog Finn chained up outside howled, and Bowser slept on the floor. The maids had been left in charge of the children and faithfully did their best. O'Neill's room was just as he had left it, never entered according to instructions laid down.

"My mother," recalls Piglet, "drove Tigger and me in the trap over to Spithead on Christmas Eve to take some presents for the children. There was much chat with the two maids who told my mother that Agnes had forgotten to leave their wages. Also she had not left any money for food. While we were there the Huber children brought their presents."

Shane confided to his friend, Peggy Ann, how he could not understand why there were no Christmas presents for them at home. She remembers teasingly saying to him, "You must have been a bad boy."

"I may have been," replied Shane, "but Oona is only two and she has never done anything bad."

"I went to Mummy," said Peggy Ann, looking back at it.

When Joe and Mary Huber realized the plight of the children next door they, in the spirit of the season, sent their butler, Foster Timoney, over to tell Lily to bring the children for Christmas Day. Timoney was a tall, good-looking chap with light skin and yellowish green eyes. The

The Ridgways went to Spithead at Christmas in their elegant pony trap.
June (Piglet) holds the bridle of the pony Molly that lived for thirty years.
(*Bermudian Magazine*)

Hubers liked him so much that they would take him back to Philadelphia when they went home for the summers. He was in his early
twenties and was a cheerful observer of the foibles of rich Americans.
Shane was embarrassed by the invitation because he and Oona had
nothing to give. He got Lily to help him to wrap up some of their old
toys in brown paper, which was all they had. On Christmas Day the
little girl, holding the maid's hand, walked over with her brother who
carried the gifts to Fleetwood Manor.

Peggy Anne recalls, "Mr O'Neill had sent a huge box of presents, but
Agnes had forgotten all about them, she had put them away somewhere."

In New York the drama of the great playwright and his wife un-
folded in harrowing encounters because it was evident there was love
still there. Agnes clearly wanted O'Neill to return home and clutched
on to the idea that their marriage was not over. She was staying in
O'Neill's hotel, the Wentworth, and when Carlotta found out she was
very angry. A quarrel ensued. In the city, friends of the estranged
couple were wooed by both sides for allegiance and sympathy. They
listened patiently to the justifications and excuses of the one and the
tearful bewilderment and accusations of the other.

With his two plays about to open and the final rehearsals taking place, O'Neill was beside himself with apprehension and worry. The theatre world was in a state of excited anticipation. Alfred Lunt, the great star of the American stage, was cast in the lead role of Marco Polo amid the music and pageantry of *Marco Millions*. Equally thrilling was the prospect of seeing the famous actress, Lynn Fontaine, in the role of Nina in the nine-act *Strange Interlude*. O'Neill's name was heard everywhere. The drama of his not-so-private life could have been written by himself. Agnes was in his hotel and he had made love to her. The children were alone in Bermuda. Carlotta was furious, and he wanted a reconciliation with her. As Agnes tarried in New York in January, Timoney the butler says Huber wondered if anyone was ever coming back for the children. The Stokes, patrician Philadelphians like the Hubers, lived next door to Fleetwood Manor on the other side from Spithead. Charlie Stokes also kept an eye on the O'Neill situation. The wolfhound Finn Mac Cool could not stand the idle *bon vivant* and barked at him. Stokes for his part got fed up with hearing the big dog howling on moonlit nights.

Finn Mac Cool, O'Neill's friend and companion, had his own opinion of that Christmas and the weeks of slim pickings. His beloved master was away and his mistress also. The big wolfhound was hungry and the foolish cackling of the large Rhode Island Red chickens was too much for him. He tore the coop apart and in a frenzy of flying feathers, squawks, and flapping wings he bit and shook until all lay dead. He was standing with a large bird hanging from his mouth when Stokes appeared. The Philadelphian Brahmin went to find the young coloured butler who sixty years later told the story.

"'Timoney I want to speak to you,' Mr. Stokes says to me. 'Come round the back.' I went round the back and he told me about the chickens.

"'I'll give you my revolver,' he says, 'and I want you to go round and shoot the dog.'

"I didn't like the idea. 'What's Mr. O'Neill going to say when he comes back?'

"'Don't worry, I'll straighten it out,' says Mr. Stokes.

"I'll never forget it. He gave me his revolver and I went round. There was the dog, standing. He was a real pretty dog, big. Mr. O'Neill brought him into the island. I shot him. It was around three in the afternoon and I took the revolver back to Mr. Stokes.

"'You kill him?' he asks me.

"'Yes,' I says. I thought for sure it was dead. Mr. Stokes went round a little after four and he came back looking for me.

"'Timoney!' he says real quiet, 'Come here! Come round the back!' He didn't want Mr. Huber to know anything about the dog. 'That dog isn't dead,' he says, 'I'll get my revolver and you go back and shoot him again. Make sure he's dead this time.'

"I thought to myself that dog was dead. I must have hit him in the head because he flopped and laid off. I went back a second time. I didn't like to do him. I shot him a second time. I made sure he was dead. It was a prize dog. Not a vicious dog. All that night I was thinking about that dog. I'll never forget it. It was the first time I ever had a gun."

The old man sighed, his brutal deed so clear in his mind's eye. He was remembering the excitement of having a gun, the older white man's persuasion, the bloody body of the dog.

Shane had caressed the rough coat of the wolfhound Finn Mac Cool for as long as he could remember. His father loved dogs, and he had been brought up to regard them as part of family life. Finn was dead. The boy's chickens were dead too. It had been his job to feed them and to collect their warm eggs. He knew each hen individually. His child's heart ached, and he sobbed over what he could not understand.

In New York the first play was ready. O'Neill was very temperamental about the opening of his plays and kept to his habit of not attending the first night. He liked to be at the dress rehearsal and then was impatient to be off to some remote spot to get on with writing the next play. *Marco Millions* with Alfred Lunt opened on January 9. The scenery was beautiful, evoking the days of the Doges of Venice and the eastern grandeur of the court of the Kublai Khan. Agnes attended the opening night with her twelve-year-old daughter Barbara. O'Neill spent the evening with Carlotta and did not go near the theatre. A few days later Agnes and Barbara sailed on the maiden voyage of the ship the Q.S.M.S. *Bermuda*.

The gala departure from the East Side pier could hardly have been in keeping with Agnes's aching and anxious heart. Crowds had come to see the new ship off. The maritime world was wishing her good luck with booming sirens. Streamers hung from her sides and the band played on deck. The *Royal Gazette* and *Colonist Daily* says, "There was an air of fantasy. The fire tugs sent long plumes of water into the air, whistles blew, and ships in the river sounded their deep throated sirens.

Marco Millions with Alfred Lunt as Marco Polo at the court of the Kublai Khan. (*Yale University*)

Small craft followed her as she made for the open sea." An exuberant welcome awaited the *Bermuda* in Hamilton. The paper reported, "Combining the very latest developments in marine engineering with only the most beautiful from the world of artistic design and decoration, the new motor ship *Bermuda* is an outstanding achievement in marine construction, a world's masterpiece of science and art."

The ship was the bright new hope for the tourist trade to the islands. "There was never such a jolly crowd ever sailed for the Isles of Rest," the press reported. Agnes had been somewhat buoyed up by the festivities. On the short ocean voyage, in the luxurious ship, ordinary life had temporarily ceased, all problems were suspended, the mind closed, just the senses living for the moment. When she and Barbara disembarked, the band was playing and flags were flying. As they drove home to Spithead no joy remained in Agnes's heart, and the full realization that she was facing a life without O'Neill and the children, life without a .father, overcame her.

Later in the January afternoon, the twilight falling, Agnes stood looking at the dog Finn's big grave where Johnson had buried him.. Lillian had told her about the bullet wounds and how no one knew who did it. Her emotions overflowed to think anyone would kill O'Neill's own dog, on whose head his hand had so often rested. He was their dog too - the family's friend. He had come all the way with them from America and had met his violent death, a brutal execution. All her sadness mingled together. The great ache for what might have been with her husband, the bereft feeling she had about the children all converged, and Finn's death became a symbol of finality. She was stunned by the realization that someone had hated Finn Mac Cool and had felt free to come on their land to kill their dog. She shivered as the darkness fell, turned away, utterly lonely.

Timoney continued his story. "The fellah Johnson came over to the Hubers, very suspicious, and asked me! I says 'Don't ask me! Ask Mr. Stokes!' Johnson took and buried the dog. He dug a big hole. When Mrs. O'Neill came back she put up a sign over him. I don't know what it said. I never went back over there for a long time. Yes, she put up a sign over that dog."

O'Neill and Carlotta eloped to France, sailing in the *Berengaria* on February 10th 1928.

The social season got underway in Bermuda, its many shining facets reflecting the diversity of the people and their interests. The ships of the Royal Navy returned from winter cruises to the south, and the officers held dances on board, inviting young Bermudian ladies and the "Fishing Fleet." The latter were English girls who came to the islands to visit relatives and friends, mostly naval and military families stationed in Bermuda—their aim to hook their future husbands. There were tennis parties and picnics at the races where the horses were ridden by young officers, mostly the younger sons of the English nobility and gentry, around a primitive track at Shelly Bay. Tourists also went to the races and enjoyed seeing the English having fun. Yacht races took place between American and Bermudian teams sailing one designs and six meter yachts, newly built in Norway. Parties were given for the visiting sailors. Spring vacations in Bermuda were becoming popular with the college crowd. The young American stalwarts risked life and limb playing rugby against the naval and military teams.

At the Mid Ocean Club, golfers played the grand course, social events were elegant and for those who wanted to relax there were the quiet beaches and coves. Important people like the Roosevelts were building houses near the Club. Dances were held at Government House, Admiralty House, by the Colonel of the Regiment, and at the hotels. There was a costume ball at the St. George Hotel.

Mothers dragged their daughters at four o'clock, teatime, to call on important hostesses. The servant opening the door would invite the ladies into the hall and proffer a small silver tray for their calling cards. If the mistress of the house was at home the visitors were shown into the drawing room where tea was on hand. Etiquette required the visit to last no more than half an hour. At official residences, calling cards were left in the hall, the guest book was signed, and the ladies were free to clatter away in their carriage. No invitations were forthcoming to Government House to anyone who had not called. No coloured people were ever invited there to social events.

Agnes did not take part in the season's whirlwind of gaiety. She was cut off by her despair and partly by habit. O'Neill had always disliked casual cocktail party chatter and considered Bermudian society a waste of time. Agnes began to dull her difficulties in alcohol and then to drown them. George Powell says she became quite ill. Lily, who had had some nursing training, took care of her. The lawyers were drafting the divorce agreement and O'Neill wanted her to sign it at once. Agnes saw no reason to hurry, for which she can hardly be blamed, and O'Neill wrote incensed letters saying he could not work until all was settled, and if she procrastinated and no writing was done there would be no money. He did not tell of the fine financial success of *Strange Interlude*, which reputedly made over $200,000. O'Neill won his third Pulitzer Prize in May for the play.

The lighthearted Hubers coaxed Agnes into their social activities. Peggy Ann remembers how much her mother liked Agnes. Slowly she resumed her writing and told O'Neill about it in her letters. From France, he replied in his tiny handwriting, "Dearest Agnes: Your two letters reached me yesterday, and I was certainly damned happy to know that you're getting down to work on a thing that deeply interests you. It gives me more satisfaction than I can tell you to hear that you are writing again and confident and happy about it. That was the news that I have been looking forward to hearing. Now you are all right and on your own feet in your own life! That is exactly what you needed! If you had that in the past few years we might have won out to final happiness together - but I realize it was exactly the fact of my being around that made it impossible for you! The irony of our fate, what? Well, when you come into your own as a writer - and I am absolutely sure you will if you hew to the line! —you can look back and bless the day I got out and left you free to do your stuff?"   .

Any compliments O'Neill included in his letters were set off by hurtful sidewinders. From France, where he and Carlotta had rented the Villa Marguerite in the foothills of the Pyrennees, he replied to her "dirty dig" when she reminded him of his "fatal criticism" of her writing in the past telling her: "Write something else." However, he said: "I shall look forward with the keenest interest to reading your scripts.... After all, you must acknowledge, if you are honest, that I have always done my best to encourage you to do your best and not to attempt easy things, or unimportant themes, or junk for money." He was at work on *Dynamo*, which he said "looks grand to me and ought to evolve into a real 'big one.'" The play would be a disappointment to him, as it was poorly received by audiences and critics, causing O'Neill to have misgivings about his idea that *Dynamo* would be the first play of a trilogy.

News of the O'Neills' separation reached Gaga in Provincetown, and she wrote a pathetic letter to O'Neill. His conscience was on edge so he appealed to Agnes:

"This reminds me: won't you please write to Gaga and give her some definite information about where she stands and what you want her to do? I've just had a letter from her and she seems in a terrible state about our breaking-up and her own future, she writes that she's heart-broken because she knows she'll never see the children again, etc. It almost made me cry, honestly. She said she hadn't heard from you in a long time. I've sent her a hundred but it isn't money she needs. God damn it Agnes, whatever her faults we've both loved her, our children have loved her, and she's loved all of us, and stuck to us since Shane was born through thick and thin, and you can't hold her idiotic gossip against her when it's a case of wounding an old woman who has been a good friend to us, if there ever was one. You can't throw her aside as if she were an old rag that you'd used up and wanted to get rid of. Won't you please do something for her? If you think I've done anything for you, then I ask this as a favour! I'll pay whatever added expense she costs you. You know I can't do anything for her. It's being near the children she loves in what for eight years has been her home. For Christ sake, please write her. It's on my conscience and I feel like hell about it."

Agnes did not hurry about this either. Under a proposed divorce agreement she would retain Spithead either to live in or if she did rent it she would keep the money. If she remarried, the house would be made over to her two children. She would receive $9.000 a year out of which she had to pay school fees. When O'Neill got angry he wanted the house to revert to him, after all it was his house, and $500 a month was all he would give her, He would pay the school fees. O'Neill consistently wanted the best schools for his children and was about to see Eugene Jr. through Yale. He wanted Agnes to remember he was a playwright and not a business man and therefore his income could vary tremendously. He had $45,000 tied up in Spithead, plus $15,000 in the furniture from the Ridgefield house - this was half of his entire capital. He referred to his "puny assets". When he was in a softer mood he wondered if the family could manage in Bermuda on what he proposed as he considered the island expensive, especially for food. He though they might be better off in Europe where he found the cost of living more reasonable.

Interlaced with cold legalities and iron finances were hot feelings. O'Neill wanted Agnes to understand that it was not only she who was suffering when he wrote, "For Christ sake, don't you think I suffer too? If you don't, Agnes, you're a damn fool! Sometimes—and often!— when I think of Shane and Oona I suffer like hell from a sense of guilt towards them, and a deep sense of guilt because I've made you suffer. You know damn well that I am a man who shrinks from the very notion of deliberately causing anyone sorrow. (Rages and fights and what one bitterly says then don't count)."

Oona in the winter garden at Spithead. *(Yale University)*

Referring to the children, he wrote, "I miss him and Oona like hell at times. Don't sneer! I love them as much as you—perhaps more—in my oblique inexpressive fashion. At any rate, they will find out I have been

a good father - (as Eugene did) - when they are old enough to understand all that has happened and when they really come to know me".
He even thought he might visit them at Spithead when he returned to
the States if Agnes were on a trip to New York.

In a gentle mood his thoughts turned back to happier days: "I have
my bad hours and days, naturally, but they are due to myself alone and
to my obsession with the past which will take me years to shake off....
for example, the other day I had a sudden clear vision of the day at
Happy Home when Shane was born, of my holding your hand, remember?.... It is only the poison and hate I must forget - in justice to both of
us and the nine years in which, speaking generally, we did our best.

Shane who had settled down well as a boarder at Somers College
wrote enthusiastically to his father and O'Neill replied, "I was awfully
glad to hear from your last letter that you like school so much and that
you've been going to picnics and having such a wonderful time in
general... I'm putting in this letter a check made out to Mother to buy
you a birthday present—you can pick it out." He mentioned he was
going on a long trip: "But no matter how far off I am you'll know I'm
thinking of you all day and maybe one of my thoughts will fly through
the air and you'll hear it and think of me. Let me know if you do..." He
wanted the nine year old to have his bicycle too, for his birthday. "And
for a Christmas present I give you my kayak and all the paddles and I
give to you and Oona, each to own half, the St Lawrence rowboat... And
you must take care of Oona and not let her stand up in the rowboat, and
promise to teach her how to row as soon as she is big enough. And,
above all, you must promise to look after these boats and never let them
scrape or bump on the rocks and see that they are kept painted and kept
in good condition - especially the kayak, which you must always
remember your Daddy loves so very much because he spent so very
many happy hours in it and every time you go out in it you must think
of him." These were heavy burdens for such slight shoulders. And the
bicycle? It was man-size much too big for Shane and could only rust
away in the salty atmosphere.

In October of 1928 O'Neill and Carlotta gave up their villa in the
beautiful Basses Pyrenées, made a leisurely trip to Paris by car before
starting on their voyage to the Far East. Travel was slow and the trip
would take the best part of three months. Before embarking O'Neill
wrote to his old friend Kenneth Macgowan, venting his spleen over the
delayed divorce. Agnes had accused him of "cruelty, parsimony,

drunkenness, and God knows what else." He had detectives try to dig up derogatory things from her past and accused her of being greedy and trying legally to blackmail him. He took terrific swipes at Agnes's family, calling them "bred-in-the-bone yellow liars."

In a tirade to his lawyer, Harry Weinberger, he wanted him to send private detectives to the farm in Connecticut where Agnes had been brought up. He questioned if in fact she had married Barbara's father in England as she said. But if she had, he had never seen any evidence of divorce from the man and if there had been no divorce, what did that make him? And what about his children? He did not want to hurt Barbara but he needed something to hold over Agnes' head. "Her friends have stuffed her with the idea she has me by the balls or she would never have the guts to act as she is doing," he wrote. In a desperate effort to get O'Neill back, Agnes had written to say she was pregnant after their hotel stay in New York that January but in her agitation she had put the wrong dates making it impossible for him to be the father. He had the letter. Agnes, not pregnant, was staying with an actress friend whom O'Neill considered flighty and O'Neill wanted her followed in case his wife could be caught "in flagrante", giving him a weapon to enable him to dictate divorce terms. He advised his lawyer: "As to Spithead keep it to bargain with". He was to tell Agnes, that if she would not sign what he wanted, she would not get the house.

He wrote indiscriminately to friends lambasting Agnes but the following year he regretted it. "I wrote a lot of dam fool ones to the wrong people," he wrote, "I was in an enraged and bitter state of mind... My letters were a sort of counter barrage aimed at the gossip spreaders. Childish stuff of course. I know that now - but I was all emotion then and impulse to hit back, and to explode or burst."

Meanwhile, Carlotta hoped a long sea voyage away from it all would help. In his diary O'Neill entered "Andre Lebon (sailed from Marseille for Hong Kong Chine)." He worked almost every day on the two month voyage. The ship stopped at many ports and he often found a pool at some hotel and went for a swim. In those days no pool was part of a passenger ship's construction but when the vessel reached the tropics a canvas pool with running salt water was rigged in the well-deck for the passengers to have a cool dunk and swim a few strokes. If the ship crossed the equator King Neptune presided over some serious dunking. Towards the end of the voyage O'Neill became ill and run down with flu which he could not throw off.

By the time they reached Shanghai, his mood had swung round to a feeling of morose guilt for walking out on Agnes and his children. There is an account of how he went on a drinking spree. He had for a companion a reporter called Batson whom he had known in Provincetown and had run into on a street corner in the Chinese city. He fought with Carlotta and hit her. "Took a poke at Carlotta and she's gone. She's gone home, I guess, but I don't give a damn," he told Batson. That night they went to a dance hall. Hours later the playwright and the reporter, both well liquored, made their way out of the dance hall, but at the curb O'Neill crumpled down and, started to weep, said, "Did I ever tell you what a son of a bitch I've been to Agnes? No, well it's true and I'll tell you all about it." Writing to De Polo later on O'Neill does not mention this episode but wrote "So when we got to Hong Kong, my destination, I was too sick to go ashore. At Shanghai I went to a hotel —and to bed. Then the newspapers got on my trail and every other busybody in Shanghai. The Anglo-American colony there is like a rotten small town. My nerves were sun-shattered and gone and I still had the flu. The doctor fearing I was going to crock completely, ordered me to the hospital where I spent two weeks. And that's how the reports of my dying came to be cabled to God's country."

Until Shanghai, the press had had little to report of the continuing saga of the great dramatist's desertion of his wife and children and his romance with the beautiful actress. When writing postcards to the children in Bermuda he never put an address or disclosed further destinations.

After his trip to the Far East, O'Neill's rage against Agnes was prompted by an indiscretion she committed, when she was at at her family's modest summer house at Point Pleasant, New Jersey. She was there making improvements, for it was going to be home for her and the children in America. Reporters seeking the latest on the scandal hounded her. She indiscretely gave an interview, which she had promised O'Neill she would not do, to the *New York News*. The headlines blazoned that she was going to grant O'Neill his "illusion of freedom." O'Neill was very angry and never wrote to Agnes again. His attitude towards her changed from one of persuasive reasoning to violent hatred. The war of words that had blistered in the mailbags sailing back and forth across the Atlantic ceased. The many thousands of the words they wrote to each other when apart, during the years of marriage, now lie in libraries, boxed, catalogued, numbered, temperature controlled. The verve of living and the human feelings spring from the aging pages. The neat, small handwriting, line after line, page after page, reveals O'Neill on the one hand, and Agnes's round calligraphy on the other hand tells its story.

Tank
'Spithead'

J B Wakers

Chapter 9

The family lives at Spithead and in Point Pleasant, New Jersey.
Agnes gets a divorce.
Shane at school in the U.S. shows first signs of instability—drinks.
Oona at Breerley spends her summer in Bermuda and, at eighteen, elopes
with Charlie Chaplin and is disowned and disinherited by O'Neill.
The playwright jubilantly remarries and lives for two years at Château du
Plessis, writing *Mourning Becomes Electra*.
They return to the U.S. and build a house at Sea Island, Georgia.
O'Neill writes *Ah, Wilderness!*
They move to California and build Tao House, where the early signs of
crippling disease appear.
The playwright is awarded the Nobel Prize for Literature. He is deeply
affected by World War II.

In Bermuda the little household, bereft of O'Neill, became Agnes's sole
responsibility. The children had had a rough time, especially Shane,
and it was up to her to smooth the path of life for them. The acrimony
of the past months had taken its toll and she tried hard to keep her
equilibrium. In spite of her press interview she still resisted signing the
divorce papers. Perhaps her husband would come back-get tired of
Carlotta and travelling. She could not believe he was gone for good.

Meanwhile she would finish those renovations to Spithead that were already under way. Shane continued his schooling at Somers College as a boarder where, his classmates report, he was very well liked. O'Neill wrote to him often and shorter letters to Oona, sending photographs of himself so they would not forget him and wanted more of theirs to put up in his study where he saw them everyday.

A blow came particularly for Shane with the news of Gaga's death - yet another anchor from his earliest youth gone. O'Neill was upset too and paid tribute to her, writing to Weinberger, "I loved the old woman! She was grand to us in our early years when I had nothing—loyal as hell to us! There is nothing I wouldn't have done for her! When Agnes cast her off last spring it was I who shamed her into taking her back. I sent money then to Gaga... A fine simple human being, generous, loyal, affectionate was Gaga!" She had truly loved the children and they had loved her in return.

In Bermuda, the island's economy was expanding as its beauty and tranquillity attracted more tourists. The Government agreed to allow an English company to build a railway and passed legislation for the compulsory acquisition of the necessary land. The horse drawn busses taken by O'Neill and Agnes into Hamilton from Campsea their first winter in 1925 were still rumbling along, the only public transport by road, linking the ends of the island with the capital. The train would provide more comfortable and faster transport than by road, and offer scenic views, from one end of the island to the other for the tourists to enjoy. They could take their bicycles on the train, get off where they liked perhaps to explore St. Georges or the magnificent beaches along the south shore. Moving heavy weights by horse and cart had become a real problem and the train would partly solve this by carrying freight to both ends of the island. Most importantly, the unique absence of cars could be maintained and the importation of motorised vehicles could be avoided for many years.

From Spithead a terrible sight was seen at night when the fine ship the Q.S.M.S. *Bermuda*, in which Agnes and Barbara had travelled on her maiden voyage, caught fire along the wharf in Hamilton and soon became a flaming threat to the city. From her waterfront Agnes and her household watched the awesome sight of the burning ship. To save the city the *Bermuda* was towed way from the quay, her seacocks were opened and she sank in the harbour. Older ships resumed the service back and forth to New York. To replace the *Bermuda*, the Furness Line built two new ships to the highest standard, the *Monarch of Bermuda* followed by the *Queen of Bermuda*.

In the summer of 1929 Agnes agreed to sign the divorce agreement and went to Reno, Nevada, where she spent some weeks to establish a residence in order to obtain a divorce under the laws of the state.

While Agnes was trying to plan the future of her children in Bermuda and America, over on the other side of the Atlantic, in France, O'Neill confided his jubilation to his diary: "Cable that divorce granted Reno yesterday. At last, thank God! Cheers!" He and Carlotta had been to Paris to make arrangements for their marriage under French law so all being in order they returned there on a short trip and were married in a civil ceremony. They had been living for the past month in the Château du Plessis which they had rented for three years. O'Neill's study was in a *tourelle* ,where he had a peaceful view of the French countryside which he described with enthusiasm to an associate: "all sorts of grand woods and farm land—a fine old château with wonderful old carved wood furniture, including choir stalls originally from Langeais, ancient tapestries in the rooms downstairs—in short, it is quite perfect, and most important for me (inside) a great peace and calm broods over it all... There is no life around but the life of the big farm that is part of the estate—cattle, sheep, ducks and chickens, wheat and hay fields." He got along well with his landladies "three sisters of the old provincial noblesse—the Vicomtesse of Something, the Marquise of Verdun, and another—really charming people when they get to know you and find you're not all barbarian, and seemingly quite pleased to have a writer for a tenant. They feel, I imagine, that it's a bit disreputably thrilling..."

O'Neill was gratified at that time to be appreciated in Europe as a writer, and commented, "My reputation over here—in Scandinavia, Russia, Hungary, Germany, Czechoslovakia, France and England is growing all the time—many productions all over in repertoire—not much money in it, of course, but real artistic appreciation." He settled down at the château to write the great trilogy *Mourning Becomes Electra*, which evolved from his study of Greek plays and was adapted from the legend of Orestes.

To complement their aristocratic residence, O'Neill and Carlotta ordered a smart car, a Reinastella Renault, to be delivered to the castle. Always fond of dogs, O'Neill had a prize dalmatian, Silverdean Emblem, sent from London. White with black spots, this breed of dog is capable of running great distances. They were used to protect coaches and carriages in the days of highwaymen by running alongside and are sometimes called coaching or carriage dogs. A month later he got a fine sporting dog, a Gordon setter. The dalmatian, called Blemmie, became a much-loved pet, for many years a member of the family. His master and mistress ordered his accoutrements, the Gelbs record, specially made for him by Hermes in Paris; collar, leash, overcoat and rain coat. When the dog died many years later in California, O'Neill wrote a touching piece called "The Last Will and Testament of an Extremely Distinguished Dog." One thousand copies were printed in Holland on vellum and bound in the finest gray leather and given to friends. There is no indication that O'Neill ever learned of the terrible death of Finn Mac Cool.

During the rainy winter of 1931, O'Neill wrote to Shane and Oona from Le Plessis thanking them for the books they had sent him for Christmas. He enquired of Shane, "Do you like boarding school in Bermuda? Do you think it is a good one to prepare you for going to college? I know it is an early date to be thinking of this, but still you cannot start soon enough in the right direction. I think you should go to a good prep school in the States when you get a little older. I am glad you have a bicycle.... Thank you ever so much for the two snapshots you sent me. You are certainly growing big and so is Oona. I shall put the pictures in a frame and keep them in my study so that I will always know how you look now and not the way I remember you. All love to you both. I'll write to you again before long. As ever, Daddy"

Through the years the O'Neills invited many distinguished visitors to enjoy the elegant delights of the château. Many of them were new friends from the theatre world. Sadly Kenneth Macgowan and Robert Edmond Jones, old friends and theatre associates for so many years, were not liked by Carlotta and were not close to O'Neill after he and Agnes were divorced. Eugene, Jr. who was nineteen and a brilliant student at Yale went over for a fortnight's visit. Oona, Shane and Carlotta's daughter Cynthia were considered too young to make the voyage alone and were not invited. O'Neill, in his mid-forties, was handsome and physically fit, partly due to the swimming pool he had put in at the château. He decided on a youthful fling and bought a Bugatti. In this sports car he raced joyfully about the French countryside. Carlotta was terrified when she went with him for a ride because he went about ninety miles an hour down the narrow country roads. He claimed it was quite safe as there was so little traffic in the French *campagne*. He and Carlotta did a tour of Spain in the Reinastella stopping at the Ritz in Madrid, considered the finest hotel in the world. Life may have been in the grand manner which O'Neill said was what he always wanted, but at heart he was a man of simple tastes. The long dreary winters and the damp cold springs were not to his liking and in his adult life he, the Sea Mother's Son, had never lived so far away from the sea.

In dedicating *Mourning Becomes Electra* to Carlotta, the dramatist tells of the grim country where the writer of tragedy dwells: "In memory of the interminable days of rain in which you bravely suffered in silence that this trilogy might be born - days when I had my work but you had nothing but household frets, and a black vista through the salon windows of Le Plessis with the black trees still dripping, and the moist wraiths mourning over the drowned fields or days when you had self-forgetting love to greet my lunchtime, depressing such preoccupations with a courageous charming banter on days which for you were bitterly lonely, when I seemed far away and lost to you in a grim savage gloomy country of my own, days which were for you like hateful boring inseparable enemies nagging at nerves and spirits with intolerable ennui and life sickness which poisoned your spirit."

Across the Atlantic, Agnes and Oona lived most of the time in the sunshine of Bermuda, at Spithead. When Shane bicycled home from school at weekends or holidays Peggy Anne came over and he visited next door at Fleetwood Manor. Lily still worked for Agnes and Lily's son Eugene Hackett whom she had christened Eugene after O'Neill says his family thought Agnes was a movie star. He still treasures the autograph book he has with the O'Neill signatures in it. Old time Bermudians used to use many nautical terms in their everyday speech and one observer, remembering far back, said: "Agnes had a nice little cut (to her jib) used to dress nice and she looked all right - I tell you. My grandfather Ed Waldron built boats at Spithead around 1900 and he brought down the big stone blocks he cut from the cliff along the road, for the wharf - 18' x 14' one block to a horse and roller to put it in position." Bolly Powell came in his boat to take the family sailing.

On a lovely day Oona and Josephine Darrell were spending the afternoon at Fleetwood Manor with Peggy Anne. The parents were out. In Huber's bar were hundreds of miniature bottles of liquor and his venturesome daughter got the idea to set up a roadside stand. No lemonade! The little girls in their summer frocks waved to cyclists and carriages offering a taste of Cointreau or perhaps Drambuie. Josephine says Oona enjoyed the merriment and her eyes sparkled as she shyly watched the fun. Bermuda's liquor laws were flouted; luckily no official turned up and a good time was had by all.

Stonemason using two saws at once in quarry. (*Bermuda Archives*)

As she got older, Oona learnt to ride, and Agnes got her a pony. As there were still no cars, a young girl could safely trot along Harbour Road on her way to visit friends. An old gentleman says, "I often saw her dashing along - pigtails flying in the wind." It was not uncommon for girls who had pony carts to drive themselves quite long distances to school. Once there the pony was taken out of the shafts tied to a tree, watered from a bucket, brought from home for the purpose, and stroked by the girls, given a nose bag of oats at lunch time with more pats and strokes, hitched up after school and away home! School bus? Unheard of.

Agnes, thanks to the Hubers, was going about socially and getting back to her writing when she had a piece of luck. It had nothing to do with romance. The man she had lost was bigger than life and the void he left none could fill. O'Neill was not a man to get over, perhaps ever, but rather someone to mourn with an unending feeling of loss. Her luck was of a practical nature: the Miller family from Canada rented Spithead for the school year. Col. Miller played golf everyday when at home on his own course in Nova Scotia, and once a year made a pilgrimage to the Royal and Ancient course at St. Andrews in Scotland. Spithead was conveniently situated between the Riddells Bay and Belmont courses. Also it was within bicycling distance of Somers College where the Miller boys would go to school.

Although there was no direct communication between Agnes and O'Neill, all mail being channelled through Weinberger, plans were afoot for Shane to leave his school in Bermuda. It would be a big uprooting for the young boy who had already suffered several hard blows in his short life. Although Shane had spent summer holidays at Point Pleasant, to leave his friends and enter an American school where he knew no one, would be very hard. For Shane's future stability it might have been better to have waited until he was a bit older. O'Neill himself had been sent to boarding school at the age of seven while his actor father and mother toured the country. He wanted Shane to enter a good prep school. After visits and interviews the prestigious school, Lawrenceville, not too far from Point Pleasant, was decided upon. Arthur Miller writing about O'Neill says "Belying the usual characterization of him as a total loner is the large number of letters he wrote to his children. And there is no more painful irony to contemplate in all the events of his life than the way his own "cursed" family evolved."

O'Neill, over in Europe, felt it was time to return to the United States. The years of work on *Mourning Becomes Electra* were over and the manuscript in the hands of the Theatre Guild in New York. His marriage was a *fait accompli* and his private life no longer a reporters' besieging scandal. The lease was up on the Château du Plessis. Before leaving they made a tour from Lisbon of the Canary Islands and cruised along the coast of Morocco. Finally they said good-bye to France sailing with Blemmie in the S.S. *Statendam,* in May of 1931.

The return to New York for O'Neill was a time to see his old friends and to plunge once more into the theatre world. *Mourning Becomes Electra* was to be produced and would open that October. The casting of the play, revisions of the script during the weeks of rehearsals, and the arrangement of the scenery kept him tied to his desk and the theatre. Summer was approaching and he and Carlotta took a house in Northport,

Long Island, into the autumn.

Following his usual dislike for opening nights O'Neill disappeared to Northport for the opening of *Electra*. The play is even longer than *Strange Interlude*, taking six hours to perform divided by a dinner interval. Its success was overwhelming. O'Neill was heaped with praise by the critics. Newspapers and magazines outdid each other in high flown expressions of admiration. He was raised above all contemporaries. Nothing like it since Shakespeare they said! The play was divided into three parts, "The Homecoming", "The Haunted" and "The Hunted". It was a tragic story of murder and suicide set in New England. Later, it was made into a movie. (The legends of ancient Greece meant nothing to a man seen putting up a sign outside a movie theatre in Mineola, Long Island, which read "A.M. Becomes Electra!")

In the holiday atmosphere of the farm at Northport the O'Neills invited Shane to come to stay for a night. Eugene, Jr., still at Yale, had obtained the required permission from the University to get married. His father did not attend the wedding but invited Eugene and his bride, Elizabeth, to visit at Northport. Shane was able to meet his half-brother's new wife.

In the autumn Carlotta and O'Neill moved back to New York, taking a large apartment on Park Avenue as they planned to make the city their home. Carlotta's daughter Cynthia who had lived with her grandparents in California for many years came east to go to a New England boarding school. Oona, who had not seen her father since he left Bermuda, came with Shane to the city. O'Neill and Carlotta had all the children for lunch and took them to the Museum of Natural History. The O'Neills had a new Cadillac and unfortunately Oona became car sick and threw up on the new fur rug, the passengers, and the car.

The dramatist was not long in finding the city an intolerable place to live. On a visit to Sea Island, Georgia, they were greatly taken with it. They bought land and decided to build. An elegant Spanish style house, with a red tiled roof, was constructed among the pines bordering the beach. They called the house Casa Genotta, a shortening up of Gene and Carlotta. On a trip there to see how the building was progressing O'Neill wrote, "Carlotta overjoyed about house—is working on it harder than any laborer up there!" After six months when it was finished he records, "We move into Our new Home! (wonderful feeling that this is the house we have built—never built one before)."

Shane travelled with Eugene Jr. and his wife Betty by ship from New

York to Jacksonville, Florida, where they were met by the O'Neills and driven to Casa Genotta for their first visit. O'Neill had resumed his interest in fishing and arranged to take his two sons on a deep-sea fishing trip. He and Shane got a six-pound bass one day while they were casting in the surf. At the new house the dramatist had resumed his routine of writing and was absorbed in a new play *Days Without End*. He was happily once again—the Sea Mother's Son—swimming, boating and fishing. Carlotta ran a perfect household and many distinguished people came to visit. They were mostly new successful friends as many of O'Neill's old chums were looked at askance by Carlotta.

The play *Days Without End* was not going well. It had to do with Catholicism, a difficult subject for O'Neill who had been brought up as a Catholic but never went to church any more. He put the play aside and with relief turned, in a lighter mood, to write a comedy called *Ah, Wilderness!* The Guild agreed to produce it and the O'Neills went to New York for rehearsals. When he returned to Casa Genotta he continued to struggle with *Days Without End*. The anxiety over the play put his nerves on edge and undermined his health. The doctor, he recorded, "tells me on verge of nervous breakdown—must rest 6 mos—no work—or complete collapse."

After some months of rest and every kind of exercise O'Neill could tolerate, his health improved. He walked and played tennis. Carlotta joined him in all she could. They set up a croquet lawn and played with neighbours and Shane when he came to stay. As soon as O'Neill was able to get back to work he started on what would occupy him for years to come, *The Cycle*. It was to be a series of plays tracing an American family through generations of life and history from 1828. What would start out as a five play structure eventually reached eleven plays. Such a task for a man in poor health did not seem to daunt the dramatist. He worked regardless, even when "rotten nerves continue—flying out of skin."

In the evenings Carlotta organized many diversions, poker, rummy, friends for dinner, fun with the player-piano "Rosie" she had given to him.

After four years the hot, humid summers of the Georgia coast and countless small aggravations decided the O'Neills to leave Casa Genotta. Once again the dramatist was on the move. The ideal home was not so ideal after all. They travelled to the far west, taking a house in Seattle. It was from there they found a great sweep of land in the San Ramon

Valley north of San Francisco. They would build another house. O'Neill was very ill in Seattle and frequently in hospital.

It was at that time, in November of 1936, the very highest honour was paid him; he was awarded the Nobel Prize for Literature. He was still under doctor's orders to rest when the announcement was made. The rush of reporters and the avalanche of congratulations from all over the world tired him further. Movie crews hung about but he noted in his diary: "C. gets rid of them work answering letters cables nerves all shot — hell of a chance to rest cure and forget plays! — feel I am on edge of breakdown—vitality exhausted — mental jimjams". O'Neill set to work on his speech to be read at the Nobel Banquet. He was unable to go to Sweden to receive his Prize and it was presented to him in hospital in Oakland by a Swedish diplomat. With the prize came a cash award of $40,000.

Eugene, Jr. wrote congratulating him as did his old friend Kenneth Macgowan from whom he had not heard for a long time. He joked to the latter, "I'm like an ancient cab horse that has had a blue ribbon pinned on his tail - too physically weary to turn round and find out if it's good to eat, or what." He did not joke some time later in a letter to Shane who was 17 and had not written to him either about his health or about the Nobel Prize, news of which had been in the newspapers all over the country. He admonished his son, "Now if you think that is any way to act, or that I am going to stand for you acting like that and still feel any affection for you, you are badly mistaken. Oona has some excuse. She is still only a kid."

The indomitable Carlotta saw to the building of Tao House, on the beautiful land tucked into the hills reminiscent of the wine country in France. Oona had grown into a teenage beauty with fine dark eyes and a beautiful smile. O'Neill records a pleasant time when his fourteen year old daughter came to stay. He was deeply involved in writing his lugubrious play *The Iceman Cometh*, but took several days off to be with her. He and Carlotta took Oona on a tour of "Chinatown, etc." O'Neill felt lovingly toward her when he wrote "—a damned nice daughter— sorry to see her leave." It was September 3, 1939, and he adds "England, France in war—now hell starts!"

Shane, who was at a ranch school in Colorado, where he was preparing for the University of Colorado, came to stay at Tao House. At Lawrenceville he had shown a lack of stability although he started off well scholastically. In spite of great efforts on the part of the masters, he left after two years. His parents sent him for discipline to the Florida Military Academy where he managed better. He was a good looking teenager with a shy but charming manner, well liked everywhere, and all agreed he had a good mind. O'Neill was put out when Agnes persuaded Shane to give up school in Colorado and go back to Lawrenceville where he would be far behind in his studies. He could not handle it and dropped out. He would drift in and out of various activities finally taking a course at the Art Students' League in New York.

Carlotta tried to protect her husband from worry over his children even intercepting their letters, and it is doubtful if O'Neill knew to what extent Shane was using alcohol and marijuana. O'Neill, himself, tired from years of struggle writing five plays of the "Cycle", was ill. He described how he suffered with neuritis in his arm, nervous dyspepsia, low blood pressure, colds, prostate infections, woozy sinking spells, abscessed teeth and physical exhaustion.

In 1940, coming down on the ship from New York to Bermuda, Oona, now fifteen, met a cheery young man of seventeen called Don French. It was an exciting voyage as Britain and Germany were already at war, and the ship, though American, was blacked out at night. Agnes was travelling with a literary friend, Frances Noyes Hart, who had achieved some success with her book *The Bellamy Trials*. She and her two daughters were invited to stay at Spithead. Don French, on his way home for vacation, played deck tennis with the girls, and was their escort on the voyage. His family, who were Americans, had bought an old house surrounded by a great sweep of farm land and spent much time in Bermuda. He was a frequent visitor to Spithead during that summer and often arrived in his sailing boat, joining the girls for a swim. In the evening he came on his bicycle to take Oona dancing. He helped her light the kerosene lamp on the front of her bike before they pedalled off to the Elbow Beach Hotel where the outdoor dance floor overlooked the sea.

Don French describes Oona in two emphatic words, "Absolutely beautiful!" He found her a bit different from the other girls of her age and thought that it might have been on account of her father.

"Oona never said anything good or bad about her father; in fact, she never said anything at all," remarked Don. "Shane did not come down, and was considered the black sheep of the family. He had gone off the

Oona aged sixteen. "Absolutely beautiful!" *(Donald French)*

deep end." That was all the young people were told. There was no talk about Shane being into drugs and a heavy drinker.

On the soft summer evenings when the heat of the day had been blown out to sea by the breeze, another young man, Bronson Hartley, came to take Oona dancing.

"She was a lovely girl," he says, "and a great dancer. She didn't drink at all and was very adult for her age."

A retired, handsome officer of the Royal Marines remembers Oona, "To me she was the most beautiful girl in the world." When asked if he ever took her dancing, he answered regretfully, "No. I just lost my heart."

It was the era of big dance bands and wonderful dance music—"Star Dust," "Dancing Cheek to Cheek." Al Donahue before the war brought his famous band to Bermuda from the Rainbow Room at the top of Radio City. The Arthur Murrays loved Bermuda and came with their dancers, who gave lessons and had everyone dancing the tango. One young scion, diffident about being seen entering the Arthur Murray Studio on Queen Street, went into Par-la-Ville Gardens, climbed over the wall, and entered by the back door! He simply had to improve his dancing.

Bronson Hartley had to borrow a lemon from Agnes one evening when he took Oona home. His pride and joy, his carbide bicycle light was out. With a piece of copper tubing, something with zinc on it, and the lemon he amazed everyone by generating one and a half volts of electricity to get him home without a fine! The ten shillings, or $2.50, would have been a real waste of money.

How did he feel when Oona married Charlie Chaplin? "I was absolutely disappointed - absolutely!" he said. "From my point of view it was a defiling of a young girl."

The happy days of swimming and sailing and the evenings spent in dancing came to an end when Oona had to return to the fashionable Brearley School in New York. Agnes called a carriage to take them to the M.S. *Queen of Bermuda*, docked in Hamilton. Don, who came to help, says the carriage was so late they were afraid they would miss the boat. Along Harbour Road they could see the *Queen* across the water with smoke coming out of her stack.

"Can't you go any faster!" cried Oona.

"Ladies and gentlemen," replied the carriage driver, "my horse can only trot, not gallop. But don't worry," he said, waving his whip at the

The *Queen of Bermuda* docked along Front Street in Hamilton.
(*Bermuda Archives*)

Queen, "she will be back next week!"

Agnes was anxious to find a tenant for Spithead but in wartime Bermuda it was not easy. The *Queen* was soon to be requisitioned by the Royal Navy and turned into an armed merchant cruiser and the *Monarch* would be taken as a troop carrier. The American President Lines had been persuaded to provide a ship to make the run from New York to the island but many Americans did not relish the sea voyage under wartime conditions. The economy of Bermuda sank as the tourist industry collapsed. As German armies advanced across Europe, there was fear in America that Britain might be overwhelmed.

William Zuill writes in his book *The Story of Bermuda and Her People:*

"But the big change came for Bermuda when Winston Churchill, the strong pugnacious and defiant Prime Minister of Britain, and President Franklin Roosevelt of the United States agreed on the 3rd of September 1940, exactly a year after the start of the war, that the United States should acquire on ninety-nine-year leases bases at Bermuda, Newfoundland..."

Winston Churchill writes in his book *The Grand Alliance* regarding his visit to Bermuda during the war:

"... I addressed the Bermuda Assembly, which is the oldest Parliamentary institution in the Western Hemisphere. I pleaded with them to give their assent and all their aid to the establishment of the United States naval and air bases in the island, about which they were in some distress. The life of the whole Empire was at stake. The smooth working of our alliance with the United States made victory certain, no matter how long the road might be.

They did not demur."

Zuill continues:

"Troops poured into Bermuda, and construction was carried out at great speed. Hills fell before the bulldozers, sand poured ashore from the big dredgers, the shoreline disappeared, houses and trees were smashed and destroyed. It was a sight Bermudians had never seen before."

The air base was constructed at the east end near St. George's by joining several islands with rocks and sand to St. David's Island. The navy base was made in the Great Sound not far from Spithead by joining two islands to the mainland by the same method. Agnes rented beautiful Spithead to the United States Navy, and it was used as a petty officers' mess. To this day shards of Chenango pottery, which was made in huge quantities for the wartime United States Navy, are dug up in the flower beds of Spithead.

Far way in California that summer of 1940, Shane was on his best behaviour when visiting his father at Tao House for a fortnight. O'Neill had been writing the tragic story of his family in his great play *Long*

Day's Journey into Night. He relived the hopeless days of his youth in a household where his father and brother were given over to liquor and his mother to morphine. Writing about the defeat of his nearest and dearest had revived the burden of guilt he tried to forget—but never could. The dark memories broke down his health, and he was debilitated for a month. He tried to be a good father to Shane and swam with him, went for walks, and took him to a fair. When the fortnight's visit was drawing to a close, the day before Shane left, he records he had a long talk with him, and refers to his son as à "fine kid."

When Oona visited in 1941 he found her at a "silly age." Ill and out of touch with youth, he blamed "the damned New York school." Sadly, it was the last time he would ever see his daughter. Agnes was living in New York and arranged an elaborate coming out party for Oona. She was debutante number one and the press made sure everyone realized she was O'Neill's daughter. He was deeply affected by the terrible events of World II. He hated Hitler and all he stood for. He thought social frivolity most unsuitable with so many millions in travail. He was ill in bed when "news comes that Oona has become Stork Club publicity Glamour Girl—at this of all times!—I am not amused!" He could not understand her teenage exuberance and became confirmed in his opinion that Oona was a lightweight, even going so far as to note "a nitwit, I'm afraid—end up in Hollywood, I predict." O'Neill detested the movie capital. In Hollywood, however, another man had a quite different opinion of Oona when he signed her up to play in one of his films. Charlie Chaplin thought her a "luminous beauty, with a sequestered charm." She was just seventeen at the time, but Chaplin wrote, "I was confident that she was not subject to the caprices of that age." Oona married Charlie Chaplin, who was three times older than she and the same age as her father. O'Neill was furious and cut her out of his life and out of his will.

For Oona, the first years of her marriage were plagued by a paternity suit brought against Charlie Chaplin by an actress. The Chaplins lived quietly at home in Hollywood, avoiding the publicity and persecution of Charlie, until he was finally acquitted. Soon began more trouble; the press whipped public opinion against Oona's husband for alleged un-American activities and communist sympathies. Privately, they lived a life of happy devotion to each other. By the time the furore began to die down, they were weary of publicity and planned to leave the United States with their children to make their home in Europe. Oona and

Charlie had eight children, but O'Neill never saw them, and it is doubtful that he even knew their names.

O'Neill was striving to complete the play *A Moon for the Misbegotten*, which was a family piece and in a sense followed *Long Day's Journey into Night*. It was the story of his brother James, a hopeless alcoholic, whose failed life was a dark ghost in O'Neill's mind. At this time came the news of Pearl Harbor, which affected him so deeply he found it difficult to concentrate on the play. The nervous disease afflicting him, which was a puzzle to doctors but had a resemblance to Parkinson's, became acutely distressing. He declared, "would ask any Jap to kill me, and many thanks for the favour." Progressing on the play he avows he was "—eager but little done because nerves jumping out of my hands, arms—can't control." He was shaken to learn that his oldest child, Eugene, Jr., was trying to enlist in the army. He looked upon him as "a son who is also a friend!" The chauffeur who had been at Tao House for many years went off to the war, a terrible loss, as neither he nor Carlotta, who had arthritis, could drive. O'Neill tried to care for the pool, his chickens, and the almonds, but it was too much. Tao House, where he had written his great plays and spent some of the happiest years of his life, was put up for sale. He had written his last play

The trembling in his limbs, which was incurable, became worse.

Chapter 10

Tragedy and death overtake the family.
Agnes remarries.
Shane becomes a heroin addict.
The playwright completes *Long Day's Journey Into Night,*
The Iceman Cometh and *Moon For The Misbegotten.*
He becomes hopelessly crippled.

In Bermuda, right after the war the plates, some two hundred of them, left behind by the Navy at Spithead came in useful when Shane and Cathy went down for a holiday. It was not a joyous occasion as tragedy had once more struck the O'Neill family. Shane had done a short stint during the war in the Merchant Marine, and after dropping out, had worked in New York, where he met the girl he was to marry, Catherine Givens. On February 11th, 1946, their first child, Eugene O'Neill III, died at the age of two months of asphyxia in an accidental crib death while sleeping in a bureau drawer. The young couple were desperately upset by this sad event, and Agnes offered them Spithead as a change of scene.

O'Neill himself was in New York at that time. He had been trying in vain to write on a typewriter as the pains in his hands made it almost impossible to write by hand. He tried dictating to a secretary but this too was unsatisfactory. He found no machine or person could enter the quiet, solitary working habits of a lifetime. He was deeply moved by the death of his namesake and invited Cathy and Shane to dinner the evening before they left for Bermuda. Some twenty years before he, himself, had departed for the islands where his triumph over alcoholism would begin. Perhaps Shane, deeply grieved, would have a personal victory over drugs. His strong wife, with her firm sense of loyalty and love, would surely be of help. O'Neill reminisced during the evening with the young couple about Spithead saying how much he loved it, remembering the good times he and Shane had shared. He paid for their passages and sent them a hundred dollars a month while they were there. He deducted the whole amount from Agnes' alimony.

Once in Bermuda the warmth of the climate and the soft sea air did much to restore the young couple. For Cathy there was the novelty of the island with its British atmosphere, the various tones of English speech and the quaint old words used by many people. The splendour of the tropical flowers along the narrow roads, the horses, carts and carriages, the glimpses of the sea and the cheery pastel coloured houses all helped to raise her spirits. For Shane there was the pleasure of showing her the Spithead estate.

There was the gate cottage where O'Neill had written a large part of *Strange Interlude*. Up on the hill after a steep climb there were the planting fields under crops and old Scott, very much alive. People up there were glad to see Shane and would soon take Cathy to their hearts as well. The vast panorama of blue sea and islands stretching away across the Great Sound had changed. To the west the new United States Navy Base with its wharfs and huge sheds lay spread out. To the northwest the great bastion of the Royal Naval Dockyard, glinting in the sun, had remained the same. Now the western powers were hastening to wind down their facilities to a peacetime level.

Out off the dock at Spithead, where Shane had fished as a youngster, the clear shallow water shimmered in shades of aqua and *eau de Nil*. On the sandy bottom lay hundreds of empty bottles thrown there by the navy during the war. Indeed, the whole property was littered with more bottles and cans and all sorts of rubbish. Cathy and Shane were camping out in the desolate house. June Ridgway (Piglet), now grown into a beautiful young woman, heard that Spithead was unoccupied and thought it might make a wonderful guest house. She went down to look at it. The doors were wide open, nobody was about, so she wandered in. Cathy and Shane, apparently, did not go in for washing up for there in the kitchen, littering the counters and table were the two hundred navy plates—unwashed.

The young O'Neills returned to New York where they lived in acute poverty for Shane seldom had a job and his father gave him little money. Now O'Neill only communicated with his son through his lawyer, Winfield Aronberg, who had taken over his affairs when Harry Weinberg died suddenly. O'Neill was very distressed to lose Weinberg on whom he had relied for so long and writes "twenty eight years of friendship... His friendship will live in my heart as long as I live". Shane was smoking Tea, as marijuana was known then, with a group who had Tea parties! They listened to jazz and reached euphoric heights and had great lifts to their self esteem. But this was not enough for Shane eventually he turned to heroin becoming addicted. Tragic family history was repeating itself.

Soon after the young O'Neills had returned to New York, from Bermuda, Agnes, joined by Oona sailed down to put Spithead in order. They worked to make the beautiful old house into a home once more. Agnes was anxious to find a good tenant. She had been very successful with her writing. Her novel *The Road is Before Us*, newly published had been favourably reviewed by both the New York Times and the New Yorker. As soon as she finished renovating Spithead she was going to Hollywood to write a movie script from it. She was again lucky when members of the DuPont family rented Spithead for the summer.

Charles T. Wood, now the Daniel Webster Professor of History at Dartmouth College, remembers what fun it was when his family rented the gate cottage that same summer. He writes that Oona paid them a visit

> to inspect as the then owner, both Spithead and the cottage which had been an officers' club for the United States Navy during World War II, and there was naturally a good bit of wear and tear. In particular my mother was struck by the number of bottles on the bottom just off the dock, and she, knowing that my brothers and I both liked to swim under the water, got us to diving for them to clean things up.

The boys dove up bottles to fill about fifty cases "and that scarcely made a dent," continued Professor Wood:

Our conclusion was that officers must have sat on the dock of Spithead every evening, having their nightly drinks, and when they were finished, they just threw the bottles in—and some with great vigour since the area covered was truly amazing. I assume most of them are still there, though now blessedly hidden by encroaching coral.

Apparently Eugene O'Neill himself had used Spithead Cottage as his writing retreat. It had, still, a considerable library of his signed books (apparently not of interest to the Navy), and I can remember the fun we had in the evenings just looking over what was there—and then trying to figure out which works had had a role to play in some of his own writing. The only one I remember now was an obvious one: a copy of Marco Polo heavily annotated in O'Neill's own handwriting, from which it was pretty easy to see just what sorts of materials he had used when writing *Marco Millions*.

The tenants at Spithead were terribly nice, and we saw much of them all, not least because, when they discovered we had already subscribed to the Royal Gazette and Colonist Daily, they did not, but just came over every evening to borrow ours. Spithead itself was in rather better shape than the cottage but a bit sparing in its furnishings since the Navy ones were gone and the O'Neills or Chaplins hadn't done much to replace them. The only real problem that either house experienced was airplane noise. At that point, the island just across from the property was the air terminal for BOAC's flying-boats, which came in, landing on the water, from the States every afternoon around four. This was noisy, but also something of a nuisance, because I had a sailboat and, until I learned better, that was apt to be about the hour I was returning from whatever exploring I had been doing of the Great Sound or Two Rock Passage, etc..... BOAC had a speedboat that would put out from the island in advance of the flying-boat's arrival, shooing away all unwanted boats, primarily me. On days without much wind when you're right in the landing path, that can be something of an experience.

The greater problem, though, came from the United States Navy Base since, once a week, its sea planes practiced night landings and Spithead was right in the landing path. Every three-and-a-half minutes like clockwork, a Corsair would zoom over at full throttle, shaking everything in both houses and certainly depriving everyone of any possible sleep.

Certainly at times relationships had been strained between the Americans and Bermudians over the establishment of the bases but the latter were quick to realize the monetary benefit they already reaped. The establishment of a commercial airport at the east end was already taking place. A witty song attributed to two young United States naval officers, sung to the tune of Mr. Gallagher and Mr. Shean, was a sure fire hit when sung by the new Calypso group, The Talbot Brothers.

Two of these verses went:

Oh Mr. Trimingham, oh Mr. Trimingham
These Yankees are a blooming lot of bores.
We have tried all we know to relieve them of their dough
But the blighters keep coming back for more.
Oh Mr. Trott, oh Mr. Trott
We bes' not take all that they've got.
If we strip them to the peel, there'll be nothing left to steal.
Absolutely Mr. Trimingham. Positively Mr. Trott.

Oh Mr. Trimingham, oh Mr. Trimingham
What's the matter with these Yankees any way?
We have given them no land, so they sucked up tons of sand
And have added many acres to our shores.
Oh Mr. Trott, oh Mr. Trott
Now peace will put those Yankees on the spot.
We will charge a goodly fee, to replace it in the sea.
And they'll pay it Mr. Trimingham. Need I say it Mr. Trott.

Tourists were returning to the islands and Bermudians, who had mourned their dead lying buried overseas, were trying to adjust their economy to post-war conditions. The armed forces during the war had brought motor vehicles of all sorts to the island. The Government, in a dilemma, finally voted, by a majority of one vote, in favour of admitting cars and commercial vehicles. However, they would have to be of small size, low horsepower, one car to a family which could not be replaced for five years. There was to be no second-hand car market and a speed limit, strictly enforced, of twenty miles an hour, fifteen in certain areas.

Agnes, who had been alone for many years, renewed her acquaintance with Morris "Mack" Kaufman, a man much younger than herself, who was a writer involved in the movie industry. She decided to marry him. O'Neill gave her $17,000 in final settlement. She made over Spithead, the cottages and land to Shane and Oona in accordance with her divorce contract, although she continued to use the house as usual. She and Mack moved to Bermuda.

The beautiful Bermuda sea appealed to her husband and he bought a motorboat which swung on a mooring off Spithead. He took Agnes to explore for the hidden beaches on remote islands. It was an easy run to Ely's Harbour, under Somerset Bridge, to the open sea where the tropical reefs, at low tide, stand above the sea. Through the clear water could be seen parrot fish feeding on the coral and the pale anemones swaying to the rhythm of the ocean. Small brightly coloured fish darted about amid the sea fans. Bermudians at one time fertilized their fields with barrels of fish caught in shore. When Mack and Agnes became interested in fishing, the inshore waters were almost fished out and in spite of better tackle, fishing took patience and skill.

In Bermuda during the late 1940's there was a fever of interest in the wondrous world beneath the sea. Young American scientists were at the Biological Station, St. George's, an oceanographic institute associated with the one at Woods Hole, Massachusetts and the Plymouth Laboratory in England, to collect marine life to build a coral reef at the Field Museum, later called the Chicago Museum of Natural History. There was a shortage of marine scientists and the idea was to encourage interest in the sea in that huge inland city. It was hoped that the coral-reef exhibit would attract students to marine science. The U.S. Navy had a team at the station engaged in bouncing sounds off the ocean floor to find out more about the transmission of sound through water. The Rockefeller Foundation was sponsoring eye research with the help of fish eyes.

Dr. William Beebe, the marine explorer, had sparked great interest in the marvels of the deep during his research at the station in the 1930's. His descent in the tiny bathysphere to the dark depths of the ocean off Bermuda caught world-wide attention, as it was the deepest dive by man to that date. Bronson Hartley, Oona's youthful admirer, had spent his childhood summers helmet diving and collecting for the great scientist. Back from the war he started taking tourists diving in helmets to enjoy the curiosities of Bermuda's tropical reefs. The heavy helmets covered the head and neck, resting on the shoulders, and soon became weightless as the diver descended. Air came through a hose in the top from a pump on the deck of the guardian boat. A depth of fifteen to twenty feet was comfortable, and the helmet could be tipped off in case of panic and the diver could simply swim to the surface. For the first time, an ordinary swimmer could walk about on the bottom of the sea. The freedom of skin diving with masks and tanks was soon to come. Gold and jewels would be found in the miles of reefs around "the islands of a thousand wrecks." Not everyone can manage the aqualung and many tourists still enjoy diving in Bronny's helmets.

Unfortunately, the local people did not find Mack Kaufman *sympathique*. He was condemned as an ugly man and for Agnes an "any port in a storm" type husband. O'Neill had his opinion of Kaufman formed by a report in the San Francisco popular press of goings on in Hollywood and was concerned for Shane's sake. He wrote acidly to Eugene, Jr., "Not a pretty picture to have one's mother in tabloids (even out here) accused of pursuing in simple nudity a fifth rate motion picture hack writer, at a drunken party." In Bermuda poor Kaufman was overtaken by an embarrassing infection of boils, common during the warm humid weather and the same infection which had attacked Oona, as a small child, and also Gaga long ago.

"He came out in boils on his bottom," said Eugenia, Agnes's new maid. "People came out in boils," she continued, "when the blood got hotted up."

Mack's blood must have become very hot! His infection became serious for he had to go to the hospital, where the suffering man endured having his deep sores lanced. He could not enjoy swimming nor his boat for several weeks.

Eugenia Robinson's husband was yet another Eugene! The couple did not drink or smoke and tried to live by Christian principles. They became devoted to Agnes and later to Shane and his family. Agnes was distraught by her husband's illness. Eugenia was alarmed when she realized Agnes had started drinking, and saw how little she ate. Agnes had a way of endearing herself to people who worked for her, inspiring their loyalty, and with the exception of the French nurse Gaga, they loved her. Eugenia waited on her, taking up her coffee every morning and leaving it outside the door. When Eugenia developed a severe

Noel Coward bought Spithead Lodge, where he installed his two
grand pianos. (Frederick Hamilton, *Bermudian Magazine*)

toothache Agnes gave her some small white pills to take. The maid
went home and slept for many hours. She was so overcome her
husband, concerned, called the doctor, who gave the opinion the pills
were morphine.

Soon money became a problem for Agnes and Mack. Shane was in
trouble over drugs in the United States and needed funds. Agnes and
Oona made the sad decision to subdivide the beautiful property of
Spithead. The Government had no planning department, so people

were able to cut up property at will.

The Grays, an English family who wanted to settle in Bermuda, had recently arrived from the United Kingdom. They wanted to buy the main house. Britain, bankrupted by the war, had passed strict currency regulations regarding the exchange of sterling. Agnes wanted American dollars. The local authorities said that the sum for Spithead was too large to be taken out in dollars but they would allow a smaller amount should the Grays buy the gate cottage. This was agreed to and the rape was carried out, leaving the great historical house with little more than an acre around it. The O'Neills retained the hillside and farm land above. The beach was scandalously filled in to make a driveway. The sum paid was some $18,000, and Oona gave her share to her mother.

The Grays had much to do as the cottage was in bad repair and the kitchen still had an earthen floor. They renamed it Spithead Lodge. There was a small building in ruins at the gate right on the water and they rebuilt it into a tiny cottage. A few years later when they sold the Lodge to Noel Coward he used the little place as his own bedroom. He had a delightful maid who took care of his bedroom and his clothes. She remembers his nice things especially his silk dressing gowns. "He was a very perfumey man," she said and continues, "I could still smell the perfume as I walked back along the path to the Lodge."

Coward installed his two grand pianos in the big living room upstairs and society loved him and his amusing parties when he would play the piano and sing. His witty repartee tickled many an elbow and people laughed when he called his bathroom, overlooking the bay, the "loo with the view." His windows looked out over Turtle Bay and Granaway Deep and beyond. Sightseeing boats carrying tourists incensed Coward, as they went by, by announcing over their public address system, which was audible for miles around, that he had left England to avoid taxes. Bermudians never paid any tribute to England and to this day have no income tax. After a while he got "rock happy," a Bermudian expression for when the smallness of the island seems intolerable, and moved to the more primitive vastness of Jamaica.

In the United States Shane was in desperate condition, for now he was a heroin addict. He and Cathy had been desperately poor before the sale of the cottage to the Grays and he had appealed to his father for money. O'Neill rejecting him would neither see him nor help him. It seemed his father had finally wearied of the responsibilities of being a parent where first Oona and then Shane were concerned. He made it plain in a letter to Aronberg, his lawyer, "as for the letter from Shane you were entirely right in not forwarding it to me. I wish you would make it as strong as you can that he cannot ever expect money from me. He has his interest in Spithead and he must make all appeals to his mother. And he might try going to work for a change... or his wife might." Shane had been arrested for possession and came before Judge Harold R. Medina, who had been a sophomore at Princeton when O'Neill was there. The Judge later told Bowen: "He looked terrible, down and out, dishevelled, dirty, dressed in rags. I felt the deepest sorrow for him, he looked so lost, so bewildered." As no one would put up the $500 bail, Shane went to jail for ten days where he suffered the pains of withdrawal until he could go to the rehabilitation centre the sympathetic Judge had ordered. He and Cathy now had a daughter Maura. When he had completed his cure, Agnes brought all three to Bermuda and installed them in the eighteenth-century kitchen cottage next to the main house. Shane, unrepentant, smuggled marijuana seeds into Bermuda and when they came up he set them out in pots around the cottage.

Mrs. Gray recalls that it took some time before she and her husband realized what Shane was growing in the pots, as they themselves knew nothing about drugs. The great drug era had not dawned, and narcotics were hardly known in the peaceful isles of Bermuda. Shane was an oddity; there were plenty of drinkers in the Island but no drug enthusiasts. He often walked around with no clothes on or with scanty, ragged garments, and as the permissive society was still to come, his behaviour shocked all sections of the community.

Shane found out that Agnes' devoted maid and friend Lily Hacket had died. She had shared Shane's life since before the dreadful Christmas at Spithead when he was seven years old and his chickens were killed and Finn Mac Cool was shot. She had been with Agnes at Point Pleasant after the divorce and had taken care of Spithead through the years. Shane heard that Lily's younger sisters Dorothy and Millicent had their own dressmaking shop in Washington Lane in Hamilton. There were delightful small enterprises flourishing in the Lane at that time. All had gardens in the back, and bananas and flowers could be seen growing beyond the windows and doors at the rear.

"I was ironing something," said Millie, "I looked up and there was this shabby young man standing there. I didn't recognize him at first but then I realized it was Shane! He was so glad to see us. We talked about old times. We had heard he had been before the magistrate in the States."

Up on the hill above Spithead there was a vacant small farm cottage. It stood at the head of a shallow valley stretching for five acres. The deep earth of the fields was a dark, rich red. The feeling up there was one of remoteness. Only a rough cart track traversed the land, and a precipitous path led to Spithead far below. The great panorama of sea and islands stretched to the horizon. Behind some trees to the south was Cedar Hill where some coloured families lived in distant cottages and it was there that Eugene Robinson had just built a house, himself, for Eugenia and their children. It was decided that Shane and Cathy should move up to the cottage in the fields. Shane took advantage of the agricultural land and soon had an impressive stand of marijuana growing. They took up Maura's battered pram, and Shane built a double bed out of planks with a bookshelf at the head. Eugenia said it was a Hollywood bed. Cathy was expecting a baby again.

George Powell, although a mason by trade, did odd jobs for Agnes, who was much loved by the coloured people. "Shane gave my mother a plant! She didn't know what it was," he explained. "She took this tree home and planted it. We had outdoor toilets in those days. Ours had a pit round at the back, and she put it there. It grew right there in that pit, big. Shane picked the large leaves off and dried them."

"People used to come there from the States and get the stuff," Powell continued. "He met them in town and brought them to Cedar Hill. You could see they were doped up people. They didn't act normal. We saw how stupid they were doing, going up to each other hugging and all that. They used to come and take the stuff away."

Powell says the cottage, where Cathy and Shane lived, was "pretty good", but "it got worse." It was a cruciform cottage with a chimney and small bake oven in the kitchen. Water was drawn in a bucket from the tank outside. A wooden tub stood on the boxes in the yard for washing clothes. A shy privy sheltered under the cedars where old newspapers were put and used for toilet paper.

On the night the baby was born it was raining heavily. Doctor Ashdown, a young doctor who had recently set up practice, recalls a small boy shiny with rain coming to the door to say that Cathy was in labour. With a flashlight he followed the boy along rows of sodden potato plants. He hurried, slipping in the wet earth, fearing what he might find.

"As I entered the room," he said, "there was Cathy sitting up in bed freshly dressed holding a baby. The room was neat and clean. The only light was a bare bulb on the end of a bamboo pole, which hung suspended from the ceiling, cantilevered with a stone tied to the other end of the pole." A coloured midwife who lived on the hill had come in, delivered the baby assisted by Shane, attended to the mother, changed the bed, and washed and dressed the infant. There was little for the doctor to do. The baby, whose name was Sheila, had been given her clothes by the kindly folk nearby.

In the late 1940's Bermuda was a haven for many struggling young writers as well as a mecca for those already famous. Constantine FitzGibbon who was writing The Arabian Bird was teaching at the Saltus Grammar School to eke out a living. His wife Theodora, an actress, got a job on the Mid Ocean News and later wrote an amusing account of those post-war days, in her book, *Love, Lies a Loss.*

She tells how Cleon Throckmorton and his wife Julie had rented a house for the winter called Angel Steps, not far from Spithead. Throckmorton had known O'Neill since the early days of the Provincetown Players. He had become a well known set designer and had worked with Robert Edmond Jones on the designs for O'Neill's plays. He had befriended Cathy and Shane during their hard times in New York. When *The Iceman Cometh* opened and no tickets were forthcoming from O'Neill, Throck, as he was called, took them as his guests.

The Throckmortons, along with the rest of the American community in Bermuda that winter were not long in hearing the news of Shane's antics at Spithead. They were acquainted with the kindly Catholic priest, Father Tom, who had heard Shane was "eating practically nothing and drugging." The priest wanted to see if he could help Shane and asked the bright and friendly Theodora to go with him. Being a man of the cloth, and knowing the O'Neill family were not close to the church, he thought Shane might be more approachable if she went with him.

Theodora was sorry she could not go with Father Tom, because of an appointment, but Throck told her not to worry as he thought now it was almost impossible to help Shane. They had heard how he was pulling Spithead to pieces, peddling the furniture, family mementos and even the bathroom fixtures. Father Tom took some food over for the family. Throck told the FitzGibbons he noticed how much Eugene O'Neill had aged when he called on him just before coming to Bermuda and that he was very unwell. He hardly ever saw him, he said, because Carlotta did not approve of her husband's old friends.

Although visitors to the island went to Shane for a supply of marijuana, there is no indication that he sold it to local people in general, just to a group on the hill. A famous story is told about how he set fire to the field of marijuana when the plants died down and dried. He stood downwind of the burning field, feet akimbo, arms raised to the sky, breathing in the swirling smoke. Stories of this driven young man outdo each other. Antoinette Frith Morris, who lived in a cottage on the nearby Frith estate, said she awoke one morning and realized there was someone in the room.

"I have a gun," the man said.

"I have one too!" she replied with spirit, recognizing Shane. Her father had brought over a large auction bell which she kept by her bed. She rang it and Shane ran away. Later on she could not find her purse.

Spithead itself was empty, as Agnes's friends, to whom she had lent the house, it being too run down to rent, had left in somewhat of a hurry. The wife had been dabbling in real estate without a work permit. As Agnes and Mack were living in Mexico and did not intend to return, Cathy and Shane moved down from the cottage in the fields to the big house.

Money for the young O'Neills was again in short supply. Bolly Powell, who could remember when O'Neill had bought the house some twenty years before and his family had worked on the renovations, was concerned about Cathy and Shane and the two little girls. Hearing they had little to eat he sailed over with food his wife prepared for them. Shane still sold things. Eugenia says a set of flat silver with a crest on it went and some fine Wedgewood china. Most of the things were of little value but perhaps people felt sorry for the family or wanted something from his famous father's house. He wanted to sell the cedar tree trunk which, to this day, holds up the ceiling in the big beamed kitchen. Eugenia restrained him, fearing the beams and upper floor might collapse into the kitchen. He did manage to take out a toilet and sell that.

At night Shane would row out on the dark water under the starry constellations, brilliant at that latitude, low in the sky, seemingly almost within reach. He would stay out there very late in the shadowy star light, causing Cathy anxiety, alone in the big house with the children.

Eugenia spent the night at Spithead sometimes. "When Cathy cried," she said, "I rowed out to look for Shane, it was three o'clock in the morning. I found him after a while, a fishing line dangling over the side of the boat. He looked at me and didn't even know me, he didn't seem to know where he was. I had to coax and coax him to come back. "You have children and a nice wife. You should think of them," I said. Her husband, the tall kindly Eugene says, "I would talk to Shane and try to help him. He always listened nicely but...." His voice trailed away. George Powell says an American official arrived, and Shane left the island forthwith. He was last seen walking down Harbour Road on his way to the boat carrying a Pennsylvania Dutch chest on his shoulder. He was just ahead of being deported by the Bermuda Government.

Cathy prepared to follow Shane back home to America. There was only one difficulty, she had no decent dress to wear. The ever resourceful Powell family came to the rescue. Lucy Powell, sister to Bolly and George who helped Cathy with the little girls from time to time, made her a dress. Mary Huber and some of her friends brought new clothes for the children. Eugenia brought over a leg of lamb and cooked a farewell dinner.

The next day when Cathy was getting ready to leave for the boat, a house agent Agnes used sometimes arrived, evidently alerted by the news of Shane's departure. The agent usually wore a felt hat turned up on one side and had lost an arm in an accident long before. She was a shrewd business woman and nick-named "The One-armed Bandit." Cathy who had no coat had found one in Agnes' closet and was descending the stairs with the coat over her arm when the "Bandit" tried to wrest it away from her. Eugenia, who was in the kitchen, says she was wrapping up the remains of the leg of lamb to take home to her family when she was arrested by a shout. "Put that leg of lamb down!" the agent called out, "It is people's food. You are not to take it." (In those days nothing was wasted and maids took home potato peelings and left over scraps of food no longer of use to the people in the household and this was known as pig swill. Many poor families along with poultry, kept a pig.) Meanwhile Cathy clung to the coat protesting it belonged to her mother-in-law and she would give it to her when she got home. Thus was the departure of O'Neills' daughter-in-law and his two granddaughters, Maura and Sheila, the last of the family to leave Spithead, the house which had so fired his imagination all those years before.

In the United States, Eugene Jr. had abandoned his promising career at Yale University for a job in radio. He was sliding down the all too familiar slope of alcoholism and soon lost his job becoming more or less dependent on O'Neill. His father had never begrudged sending money to the son he loved so much and who had been, for so long a source of great pride to him, but now he explained his views to Aronberg, painfully writing, "I don't think Eugene has any idea what out financial set up is now. He doesn't seem to realise the good old days are over." He told how Carlotta had paid for the house in Maine even having to take out a mortgage. "I feel it is about time for Eugene to sit and think things over very seriously. He is nearly forty years old. And he must make up his mind he will get nothing from me and that it is necessary to find some job, and remain on that job, to plan his future. I am not well. My tremor gets worse everyday. I will never write another play and there is no use kidding myself that I will." O'Neill had been so brave for years always hoping and planning for new work in spite of pain and enduringly progressive deterioration of his body, that it must have been hard to write those last words, and admit final defeat.

It was a dreadful time for Carlotta and O'Neill when tragedy struck the family. The playwright's nervous disorder had worsened, the trembling continued in his legs, and feet; soon tremors shook his whole body. He had quarrelled with Carlotta and they had separated but she was back with him at their house in Maine when the terrible news about O'Neill's elder son arrived. The tragic news was that he had committed suicide. Writers give vivid descriptions of the grisly event. The forty-year-old classical scholar, sitting in a bath full of water, had cut his wrists in the Greek manner. He evidently changed his mind and in panic-stricken desperation reached for the telephone only to find it disconnected. He had not paid the bill. Leaving a trail of blood, he collapsed in the downstairs hall evidently in an attempt to reach the front door and attract help. He had bled to death. Carlotta observed that after O'Neill had been told about his elder son's death he did not talk about it but sank into poorer health and deeper unhappiness.

From Marblehead Carlotta wrote a letter to Aronberg as O'Neill's handwriting had become barely legible, enclosing bills and check for Eugene Jr.'s funeral expenses. She continued, "And, if Shane goes in for more stupidities - could you write to me and let me break the news with as little shock as possible. I, personally don't see why Gene should be dragged into Shane's mode of life. Of course, he has to sign papers for the sale of Spithead - but after that! If we were dead he'd have to get on somehow - let him begin now." In agreement with what Carlotta had written O'Neill also signed the letter.

After the young O'Neills had left Spithead, the rain beat in the open windows, the wind banged the doors back and forth, and cockroaches, which bred in the palmettos, invaded the house. On a night when the moonbeams slanted in through the curtainless windows the ghost of Hezekiah rattled his sword and thumped in his seaboots across the floors. In the high ceilinged rooms the few bits of dusty furniture that remained were looked down upon by the spiders high in their webs. Left to run down for years the house and gardens were in sad condition. Both Agnes and Shane needed money, and it was decided to further divide the estate, to sell the house with one acre of land, all that was on the seaward side of Harbour Road. The wooded hill of some fifteen acres would be retained including old Scott's cottage and the arable land at the top.

The Hubers made an offer. It was low on account of the dilapidation. It was accepted. The Hubers' cagey Philadelphia lawyers insisted that the whole O'Neill family sign.. The last page of the deeds to the property is lavishly decorated with colourful Bermuda stamps sporting the head of King George VI. In spite of O'Neill's trembling hand, his signature, Eugene Gladstone O'Neill, is surprisingly firm. It is the only known time that he signed his middle name. One of the witnesses to his signature was his nurse Jean M. Welton on whom he and Carlotta relied so heavily in his last years. There followed all on the same page, Agnes Boulton O'Neill Kaufman, Oona O'Neill Chaplin, Shane O'Neill, and Charles Spencer Chaplin. The latter was required to sign because he had lent Agnes $500 with a lien on the property. The price for Spithead was twenty-five thousand dollars plus the stamp duty of eight pounds, nine shillings. As Huber had paid in American dollars, the exchange control allowed the money to leave the island.

O'Neill, after the years in the clutches of a worsening disease nothing could arrest, prayed for death and contemplated suicide. He and Carlotta were living in the Shelton Hotel in Boston where he was confined by sickness. Few visitors came. He was aware he had fallen from the public eye and that his plays *The Iceman Cometh* and *A Moon for the Misbegotten* were not well received. His income was greatly reduced and Carlotta's funds had dwindled. What he hoped would be his *magnum opus* he had not been able to finish. As his trembling hands tore the paper of the *Cycle* plays, which were to have numbered eleven, Carlotta helped him and later burnt the pieces. He saved *A Touch of the Poet* and *More Stately Mansions* survived by mistake, unfinished. His great play *Long Day's Journey into Night*, the story of his family, he did not wish produced until twenty-five years after his death.

O'Neill lived for a year after he signed the Spithead deeds. It was a sad time of pathetic ill health when Carlotta nursed him with great devotion. He was physically very weak, barely able to get out of bed although his mind was still clear. He never forgot the circumstances of his birth and a feeling of guilt never left him regarding his family's tragedies. Some of his last words were, "born in a hotel room and damn it died in a hotel room." Carlotta wanted no publicity for his funeral and he was buried quietly at Forest Hills Cemetery outside of Boston.

When the terms of Eugene O'Neill's will were learnt the *New York Times* headlined that his children had been cut off. Carlotta was his sole heir and executrix. The document stated:

> I purposely exclude for any interest in my estate under this will
> my son Shane O'Neill, and my daughter Oona O'Neill Chaplin,
> and I exclude their issue now or hereafter born.

He had told Shane years before that Spithead was to be the inheritance for him and Oona. Carlotta gave manuscripts, letters and all other papers to Yale University and appointed them to be O'Neill's literary executors. The collection is housed at the Beinecke Library at the university.

The winds of change have swept over the islands of Bermuda, and political showers have attempted to wash away racial prejudice. The coloured people, now known as blacks, are still kind and delightful, but better educated and many hold major degrees and important positions. Motor traffic hurries, crowding the narrow roads, pushing over the twenty miles an hour speed limit. Along the streets of Hamilton, purposeful men in power suits, carrying briefcases, are bent on international business. No foreign banks have ever been allowed on the island. Bermudians continue to run their own banks, which now stretch around the world, dealing in huge sums, the last word in monetary sophistication. Law firms and accounting firms are fat with the tax exempt business of reinsurance. The standard of living is very high and there is no unemployment.

The bays and beaches are still dreams of beauty. Planes and cruise boats bring thousands of tourists. The large hillside retained by the O'Neills stands in its acres, pink with oleanders. The Bermuda National Trust would like to see it remain as open space, now rare in Bermuda, perhaps even as a writers' memorial park. The O'Neill family have lost the agricultural land. When Joe Powell, who was farming it, grew old he asked his friend Wilmot to take over the fields from him. Wilmot kept pigs there and paid the parish taxes. He was granted by the court under a squatter's rights claim, derived from old English common law, five acres of land. The chimney of Shane's desolate cottage, fallen into ruins, still points to the sky. The price of such a piece of land today in the 1980's would be upward of a million dollars.

Old black people sigh now for the land Agnes promised them but never legally gave. She was well intentioned but in fact she did not own the land. After O'Neill died she wrote a book about the early days of her marriage to the great American dramatist, *Part of a Long Story*. (The dust jacket subtitle says *Eugene O'Neill as a young man in love*.) As part of her divorce settlement Agnes had agreed not to write anything about her years with O'Neill nor to give interviews. But now she felt free to release her very personal and intimate memories. The book tells an invaluable story of Bohemian life in New York's Greenwich Village of its people and of the O'Neills' own passionate love in that artistic milieu that is now almost folklore. The academic world suspected some fantasy in this very human account of love and poverty.

She wrote under the names of Agnes Bolton, her maiden name, which she took back after her separation from Mack Kaufman. Any tendency towards drinking too much was long overcome. Her later years were clouded by the erratic behaviour of Shane, his encounters with the police, the breakdown of his health and the poverty of his family. He, too, ended his life by suicide, jumping from a window. The days of the little boy running on the sand at the edge of the surf in Bermuda were far away.

Oona had left the United States with her husband Charlie Chaplin to live in Switzerland. In Europe he was honoured and feted, and Oona met the famous and rich in the arts and society. They bought a large house with views of the mountains and the Lake of Geneva. They named one of their sons Eugene. Chaplin was honoured by the Queen with a knighthood. Sir Charles and Lady Chaplin came to Bermuda with their many children on a visit. People said it was something to do

Bermudian diver Teddy Tucker blows the conch shell for Annette and Christopher Chaplin. (*Bermuda Archives*)

Chaplin children in a Bermuda Easter Lily field. (*Bermuda Archives*)

Oona and Charlie Chaplin on a visit to Bermuda. *(Bermuda Archives)*

with giving some land for the road widening. They shunned any publicity, but invited Oona's childhood playmate Josephine Darrell to come with her children so they could all meet. Oona came again after her husband died and stayed at the Coral Beach Club. The two bungalows the O'Neills rented before she was born still stand there on the cliff top, part of the elegant Coral Beach Club, smartened up to house visiting members. Far below the club terrace, the waves roll gently up the beach where O'Neill ran naked in the moonlight, a hibiscus behind his ear, reciting his own poetry.

Charlie Chaplin paid a great tribute to Oona in his book My Biography: "I have the good fortune to be married to a wonderful wife. I wish I could write more about this, but it involves love, and perfect love is the most beautiful of frustrations because it is more than one can express. As I live with Oona, the depth and beauty of her character are a continual revelation to me. Even as she walks ahead of me along the narrow sidewalks of Vevey with simple dignity, her neat little figure straight, her dark hair smoothed back showing a few silver threads, a sudden wave of love and admiration come over me for all that she is - and a lump comes to my throat."

The O'Neills are becoming legendary figures in the island, still tenderly remembered by old people, any human weaknesses long forgiven. The tales of the family are told with humour and understanding. Soon there will be none to remember O'Neill floating, thinking, drifting with the tide, or none of those who came to row him back to Spithead. The O'Neills came to Bermuda for part of their long day's journey through their tumultuous lives and each will be part of the legend.